D1527463

Library of
Davidson College

Actions and Other Events

American University Studies

Series V
Philosophy

Vol. 75

PETER LANG
New York • Bern • Frankfurt am Main • Paris

128.4
P525a

Karl Pfeifer

Actions and Other Events

The Unifier-Multiplier Controversy

PETER LANG
New York • Bern • Frankfurt am Main • Paris

r18947987

Library of Congress Cataloging-in-Publication Data

Pfeifer, Karl
   Actions and other events : the unifier-multiplier
controversy / Karl Pfeifer.
     p. cm. − (American university studies. Series V,
Philosophy ; vol. 75)
     Bibliography: p.
     Includes index.
     1. Act (Philosophy) 2. Events (Philosophy)
3. Intentionality (Philosophy) 4. Agent (Philosophy)
5. Davidson, Donald, 1917- . 6. Goldman, Alvin I.,
1938- . I. Title: Unifier-multiplier controversy.
II. Series.
B105.A35P44   1989   128'.4−dc19   88-34203
ISBN 0-8204-1044-6   CIP
ISSN 0739-6392

CIP-Titelaufnahme der Deutschen Bibliothek

Pfeifer, Karl:
Actions and other events : the unifier-multiplier
controversy / Karl Pfeifer. − New York; Bern;
Frankfurt am Main; Paris: 1989.
   (American University Studies: Ser. 5,
Philosophy; Vol. 75)
   ISBN 0-8204-1044-6

NE: American University Studies / 05

© Peter Lang Publishing, Inc., New York 1989

All rights reserved.
Reprint or reproduction, even in part, in all forms such as microfilm,
xerography, microfiche, microcard, offset strictly prohibited.

Printed by Weihert-Druck GmbH, Darmstadt, West Germany

To Susan L.,
for actions and other events.

CREDITS

Section 2.2 and chapter 3 consist for the most part of material previously published as "A Problem of Motivation for Multipliers", *Southern Journal of Philosophy* 20 (1982): 209-224.

Chapter 4 is a revision of "A Consideration of Modifications to the Multiplying Account", *Philosophy Research Archives* 11 (1985): 141-154.

Section 5.4 contains material from "Time, Entailment, and Event Inclusion", *Dialogue* (Phi Sigma Tau) 23 (1981): 51-57.

Section 8.3 incorporates, with the permission of Kluwer Academic Publishers, "Thomson on Events and the Causal Criterion", *Philosophical Studies* 39 (1981): 319-322 (Copyright © 1981 by D. Reidel Publishing Company).

Excerpts from Alvin I. Goldman, *A Theory of Human Action* (Copyright © 1970 by Alvin I. Goldman) are reprinted with the permission of Princeton University Press.

Book design and layout by E. Mitchell.

CONTENTS

1

INTRODUCTION

1.1 Anscombe's Question

The philosophical dialogue on the identity and individuation of actions and other events was initiated by G.E.M. Anscombe with the following pointed question:

> Are we to say that the man who (intentionally) moves his arm, operates the pump, replenishes the water supply, poisons the inhabitants, is performing *four* actions? Or only one?[1]

It is not altogether clear why our choices in counting actions here should be limited to one or four. If the man and the circumstances in question are locatable in the real world, obviously a

---

1. G.E.M. Anscombe, *Intention*, 2nd ed. (Oxford: Basil Blackwell, 1976), 45.

lot more goes on than is made explicit, and even what is made explicit might be variously partitioned. But these sorts of questions can be postponed, for that is not what is being asked.

What we have here are four "action descriptions"[2] respectively containing cognates of the action verbs "move", "operate", "replenish", and "poison". It is taken for granted that an action answers to each of these descriptions and we are asked whether one and the same action answers to all of these descriptions or whether each description has a different action answering to it. In other words, is the function from action descriptions to actions one-one or many-one?

Of what interest might an answer to Anscombe's question be? Let us first see what its interest is for Anscombe. She herself answers her question as follows:

> In short, the only distinct action of his that is in question is this one, [moving his arm up and down]. For moving his arm up and down with his fingers round the pump handle *is*, in these circumstances, operating the pump; and, in these circumstances, it *is* replenishing the house water-supply; and, in these circumstances it *is* poisoning the household.[3]

The specific role this answer plays in the context of Anscombe's essay is that of elucidating, among other things, how act descriptions may serve to specify intentions and also how the intentions behind an act are related to one another. For example, if

2. Anscombe's term—she uses the word "description" in a very wide sense, encompassing complete sentences, dependent clauses, predicate expressions, and nominalizations. I will follow her in this, insofar as nothing hangs on the distinctions blurred by this usage. For a critical discussion of the notion of description see S. Toulmin and K. Baier, "On Describing", in *Philosophy and Ordinary Language,* ed. Charles E. Caton (Urbana, Ill.: University of Illinois Press, 1963).

3. Anscombe, *Intention*, 46.

we ask why the man moved his arm, the answer may be that he intended to operate the pump. Similarly, the answer to why he operated the pump may be that he intended to replenish the water supply, and the answer to why he replenished the water supply may be that he intended to poison the inhabitants. Anscombe's position here is that having "one action with four descriptions, each dependent on wider circumstances, and each related to the next as description of means to end...[allows us to] speak equally well of *four* corresponding intentions, or of *one* intention—the last term that we have brought in in the series."[4]

Whatever the merits of such an explanation, it is such concerns that motivate the question for Anscombe. However, there are other reasons for seeking an answer to her question, as the following passage from Monroe C. Beardsley makes evident:

Why ask this question? One might just be interested in knowing the answer, if there is one. At the very least (perhaps at most) we may discover how various possible answers connect with—require or preclude—certain philosophical principles. And there might be useful implications for other fields of thought. For example, in the philosophy of history, where it has been argued that the objectivity of historical knowledge is impugned by the impossibility of giving decisive answers to such questions about historical actions. Or in the empirical study of international affairs, where events of certain kinds are counted and their varying frequency charted. Or in the law: I am thinking of a recent newspaper report about a woman found guilty of shooting her boyfriend outside a Wildwood (N.J.) bar. She drew ten years for manslaughter, and seven years for each of the other two charges on which she was also convicted:

> (9) possession of a deadly weapon.
> (10) possession of a deadly weapon with intent to injure.

---

4. Anscombe, *Intention*, 46.

If (9) and (10) are not two distinct actions after all, then how could each be a distinct crime, deserving its own punishment?[5]

To Beardsley's example I can add another legal one that also brings in Anscombe's concern with intention. In a newspaper report concerning one James Wright convicted of second-degree murder in the strangling death of a woman, the psychiatrist who examined the accused is quoted as testifying: "In his mind the killing could well have been an act of kindness." The Crown prosecutor countered this line of defence by arguing: "Euthanasia has always been unlawful. If Wright's only intent was kindness, that begs the question: the kindness was the killing."[6]

Finally, let me give my own reason for seeking an answer to Anscombe's question. I find the question worth pursuing because the issue of event individuation it raises has relevance for the metaphysical problem of determining the ontological status of events: how we individuate events will be telling as regards the kinds of entities events may plausibly be and the position they occupy in our conceptual framework. Some modest inroads on such concerns will be made in the course of this essay.

5. Monroe C. Beardsley, "Actions and Events: The Problem of Individuation", *American Philosophical Quarterly* 12 (1975), 263.

6. Fred Haeseker, "Killer sentenced to life for 'mercy strangling'", *The Calgary Herald*, 25 March 1977.

1.2 Unifiers vs. Multipliers

Anscombe's example, the question raised, and the possible answers suggest a rough framework for classifying the various accounts of events and their descriptions found in recent philosophical literature. Some terminology appropriated from Irving Thalberg is useful here. Thalberg speaks of the approaches of "unifiers" and "multipliers" to actions and events, and so gives the dispute over how to answer questions of the sort Anscombe has posed its name—the "unifier-multiplier dispute".[7] Thus, given the scenario of Anscombe's example for what transpired on some particular occasion, those who with Anscombe would countenance the answer "one" would be unifiers. Those who insist the answer must be "four" would be multipliers. Intermediate positions might be possible, in which some but not others of the descriptions under consideration are held to describe the same event, these positions being accordingly characterizable as exhibiting a greater or lesser number of unifying or multiplying tendencies. An observation on this framework is in order. If these answers to the "how many?" question are in part theory dependent, it will be possible for theorists to agree on the sameness and difference of particular actions and events under differing descriptions and yet do so for different reasons; alternatively, they may agree on the same criteria, but differ as to what follows from the application thereof.

In the treatment of individuation which follows I concern myself mainly with the issues between unifiers and multipliers as such, and undertake to defend the unifying position against the criticisms of multipliers. Thus, I do not directly address any of the possible

7. Irving Thalberg, "Singling Out Actions, Their Properties and Components", *Journal of Philosophy* 68 (1971), 780.

intermediate positions.[8] Nonetheless, much of what I argue on behalf of unifiers against multipliers must also be answered for by those who hold other nonunifying positions—indeed, some of the multipliers' arguments are borrowed from those who seem to hold such positions.[9] An investigation of positions falling outside the unifier-multiplier dichotomy I will leave to others.

8. Some philosophers who appear to be neither unifiers nor multipliers are Beardsley, Judith Jarvis Thomson, Lawrence Davis, and Thalberg himself.

9. See for example section 5.4 below.

2

THE UNIFYING APPROACH

2.1 Davidson's Approach

Often mentioned in the same breath as Anscombe vis-à-vis the question of event individuation is Donald Davidson. Prima facie, his views on this question are the same as those of Anscombe. Certainly his treatment of particular cases is similar to Anscombe's, as the following two examples illustrate:

> I flip the switch, turn on the light, and illuminate the room. Unbeknownst to me I also alert a prowler to the fact that I am home. Here I do not do four things, but only one, of which four descriptions have been given.[1]

> That the bullet pierced the victim was a consequence of my pointing the gun and pulling the trigger. It is clear that there are two different events,

---

1. Donald Davidson, "Actions, Reasons, and Causes", *Journal of Philosophy* 60 (1963), 686 <4>. Numerals in angle brackets after citations of Davidson's journal articles indicate the corresponding pages of the reprint in his *Essays on Actions and Events* (Oxford: Clarendon Press, 1980). Some passages I quote are slightly but inconsequently different in the reprint.

since one began slightly after the other. But what is the relation between my pointing the gun and pulling the trigger, and my shooting the victim? The natural and, I think, correct answer is that the relation is that of identity....

...It is hard to imagine how we can have a coherent theory of action unless we are allowed to say here: each of these...describes the same action. Redescription may supply the motive ("I was getting my revenge"),...give the outcome ("I killed him"), or provide evaluation ("I did the right thing").[2]

The latter example and variants thereof occupy a central place in the literature because of peculiar problems associated with the kinds of acts or events that killings are.

The tendency in the writing on events has been to treat the unifying approaches of both Anscombe and Davidson as expressions of the same position, called by some the "identity thesis".[3] I believe this is entirely correct. However Julia Annas appears to hold the view that Anscombe is not claiming or is not committed to identity for the differently described actions of her pumping-poisoning example, but is in effect arguing for a weaker relation of some sort "involving essential reference to means-end chains".[4]

---

2. Donald Davidson, "The Logical Form of Action Sentences", in *The Logic of Decision and Action,* ed. Nicholas Rescher (Pittsburgh: University of Pittsburgh Press, 1967), 84-85 <109-110>.

3. Alvin I. Goldman, *A Theory of Human Action* (Englewood Cliffs, New Jersey: Prentice-Hall, Inc., 1970), 1-2.

4. Julia Annas, "Davidson and Anscombe on 'the same action'", *Mind* 75 (1976), 255-256. I say "weaker" because Annas claims vis-à-vis Anscombe's example (with action descriptions suitably abbreviated) that "we have to be able to say only that *B* is the same *A* as *C* and *C* is the same *B* as *D*, not that *A*, *B*, *C* and *D* are all the same *F*." This notion of sameness cannot be an equivalence relation; if it were, any member of the series could stand in for *F*. Annas's views are hard to square with the account in Anscombe's later paper, "Under a Description", *Noûs* 13 (1979).

I do not intend to debate this point here. Whatever we say about Anscombe, the relation Davidson has in mind in the discussion of his examples is definitely *identity*, the equivalence relation. Furthermore Davidson has provided what he thinks is a criterion for this identity between events, namely,

Events are identical if and only if they have exactly the same causes and the same effects,[5]

or more formally,

$x=y$ if and only if $[(\forall z) (z$ caused $x \rightarrow z$ caused $y)$ & $(\forall z) (x$ caused $z \rightarrow y$ caused $z)]$.

Since the intellectual debt to Anscombe for raising the issue of event individuation has been acknowledged and she has been duly credited for originally advancing the unifying approach, I propose now to abandon further discussion of Anscombe's views and direct my attention to Davidson as representative of the unifying approach. In so doing we will avoid the exegetical concerns alluded to above. Aside from this expediency, I think this move is justified on the grounds that the relevant literature on event individuation has treated what I am calling the "unifying approach" as an identity thesis and has in fact addressed itself to Davidson's arguments for the most part.[6]

5. Donald Davidson, "The Individuation of Events", in *Essays in Honor of Carl G. Hempel,* ed. N. Rescher et al. (Dordrecht-Holland: D. Reidel Publishing Co., 1969), 231 <179>. A discussion of problems faced by this criterion will be undertaken later.

6. This is perhaps because it is difficult to discern any arguments supporting Anscombe's individuation claims at all, as Goldman not unjustifiably insinuates in "The Individuation of Action", *Journal of Philosophy* 68 (1971), 765.

2.2 Three Major Objections

Alvin I. Goldman and others have presented arguments which, if successful, would establish that Davidson's claims of event identity in his treatment of particular cases are untenable.[7] These arguments, given the nature of the objections they raise, can be characterized as being of three kinds. In what follows I will present a representative argument of each kind.

First, let us consider an argument which suggests that some of Davidson's identity claims are at odds with his own criterion. Proceeding in respect of Davidson's shooting-killing case above, this argument would assume the following shape. Consider Donald's act of pulling the trigger, his act of killing the victim (hereafter known as "Alvin"), and the event consisting of the gun's firing. Clearly Donald's pulling of the trigger causes this last event. That is to say,

(1) Donald's pulling the trigger caused the gun's firing

but

(2) It is not the case that Donald's killing Alvin caused the gun's firing.

Thus,

(3) $(\exists z)$ (z = the gun's firing & Donald's pulling the trigger caused z & $\neg$ Donald's killing Alvin caused z),

which in virtue of the criterion entails

(4) Donald's pulling the trigger $\neq$ Donald's killing Alvin.

---

7. See Alvin I. Goldman, "The Individuation of Action", which presents all three of the objections I sketch below; also see Lawrence H. Davis, "Individuation of Actions", *Journal of Philosophy* 67 (1970).

In this pattern of argument, premises like (2) are usually supported by claiming that it seems false, sounds odd, or would be counterintuitive[8] to say that

(5) Donald's killing Alvin caused the gun's firing.

Sometimes this claim of irregularity is bolstered by the claim that, if true, (5) would commit us to holding that Donald killed Alvin before the gun fired. If so, this certainly would create problems for (5). For it clashes with the presumption that it was after all (though perhaps not only) the gun's firing that did Alvin in, and with the "truism" that effects do not precede their causes.

The argument just sketched we will henceforth call the "causal argument" or the "causal objection" against Davidson's unifying approach.

Now let us consider a second argument against Davidson. A fact which is supposed to be troublesome for a unifying approach is that we often speak of one act being done or performed *by* doing another, or done or performed *in* doing another, where the italicized prepositions might be taken to express a relationship that obtains between acts. Goldman calls this relation the "by-relation". Thus, we might comment on Davidson's light-switching case quoted above that the agent (hereafter "John") who flipped the switch and turned on the light, turned on the light *by* flipping the switch. Here are Goldman's comments on this case:

> The relationship in question might be expressed by saying that the one act is a "way" or "method" by which the other is performed. Typically, when act *A* is the "way" by which act *A'* is performed, we can *explain how* act *A'* has been performed by citing act *A*....
>
> The important point to notice about this relationship is that it is both *asymmetric* and *irreflexive*. Consider first the matter of asymmetry.

8. E.g. Goldman, "The Individuation of Action", 765.

> If agent S does act A' "by" doing act A, then he does not do A "by" doing A'. John turns on the light *by* flipping the switch, but he does not flip the switch *by* turning on the light....
>
> The irreflexivity of the relationship can be seen in the same examples. We would not say that John turned on the light by turning on the light....[9]

The argument against the putative identity in Davidson's example which these considerations are supposed to buttress might then be reconstructed as follows:

(a) Any acts A, A' are identical only if the relations that hold between them are equivalence relations.

(b) The by-relation is not an equivalence relation.

(c) Therefore, no acts standing in the by-relation to one another are identical.

The upshot of this argument, if successful, is that most of Davidson's particular identity claims would be defeated, since prima facie the actions claimed to be identical would appear to be such that the one is done by doing the other.

I will label this second line of reasoning the "relational objection" against Davidson's position.

Finally, let us take up the third argument against Davidson. A possible problem concerning temporal order was hinted at at the end of the presentation of the causal objection above. Again using the shooting-killing example, a more explicit objection involving time can be formulated as follows.[10]

Suppose that Donald shoots Alvin at noon and Alvin dies of the gunshot wound at midnight. In any court of law, it would be ac-

9. Goldman, *A Theory of Human Action*, 5.

10. See Goldman, "The Individuation of Action", 767-768.

cepted as true that Donald killed Alvin. But while it is obviously true that Alvin's death occurs twelve hours after Donald shoots him, it seems false to say that Alvin's death occurs twelve hours after Donald kills him. Thus the shooting and the killing must be distinct, since the one event seems to have a property the other lacks. The shooting but not the killing precedes the death by twelve hours. This last objection let us dub the "temporal objection".

We thus see that for the examples considered the three lines of attack that have been sketched provide a strong challenge to a unifying approach to event individuation. If these three kinds of argument and variations thereof can be successfully applied to all unifying identity claims made in the context of particular examples, it would suggest that there is something fundamentally wrong with that approach to individuation as presented thus far. But if a unifying approach seems to fail, how do the alternatives fare? Can a multiplying approach meet these objections without engendering new difficulties?

Of course, while a simple denial of the troublesome identity claims in Davidsonian examples would avoid the alleged problems above, there is another consideration which cannot be handled merely by a recommendation for a multiplying procedure. The actions and events in Anscombe's and Davidson's examples are after all not totally unrelated. No matter how we count events, there is a "unity" among the events in these examples which must be accounted for. But if the relation providing this unity is, as multipliers contend, not that of identity, then another way of relating such events must be provided.

In the next chapter we will examine the multipliers' response to this challenge.

3

THE MULTIPLYING APPROACH AS ALTERNATIVE

3.1 Goldman's Account

Let us then see what a multiplying approach has to offer. Goldman and Jaegwon Kim are the chief proponents of such a position in the literature, and their positions on the ontological nature of events seem to be substantially the same. In this and succeeding chapters, I will take Goldman's views to be representative of the position and will bring in Kim only where he might be required to improve on Goldman or where he addresses himself to points not considered by Goldman.

The underlying rationale for the multiplying approach has its source in the commonplace observation that events often appear to involve, and can be characterized as the loss, acquisition, retention, or having of properties by an object at a time.[1] This observation is taken to lead "naturally" to the conception of events as ex-

---

1. See Jaegwon Kim's introductory remarks in his "Events as Property Exemplifications", in *Action Theory*, ed. M. Brand and D. Walton (Dordrecht-Holland: D. Reidel Publishing Co., 1976), 159.

emplifications of properties by objects at a time. The following passages from Goldman spell out this view;[2] first the terminological distinctions:

> I begin by distinguishing between *act-types* and *act-tokens*. An act-type is simply an act-property, a property such as mowing one's lawn, running, writing a letter, or giving a lecture. When we ascribe an act to an agent, we say that the agent exemplified an act-property (at a certain time). When we say, for example, "John mowed his lawn," we assert that John exemplified the property of mowing his lawn. Mowing one's lawn is a property because it can be *true of*, or *exemplified by*, a particular object at a particular time. Normally philosophers tend to apply the term "property" to such things as being six feet tall, being a bachelor, or having red hair. But we need not restrict the term "property" to *static* properties. Just as *owning* a Jaguar is a property that can be exemplified by John at time *t*, so *buying* a Jaguar is a property that can be exemplified by John at time *t*.

Then the criterion of identity:

> Since an act-token is the exemplifying of a property by an agent at a time, it is natural so to individuate act-tokens that *two act-tokens are identical if and only if they involve the same agent, the same property, and the same time.*

It is sometimes useful to represent Goldman's act-tokens via a notational device employed by Kim,[3] viz. [x, P, t], where x is an object or agent, P is a property, and t is a time or time interval. Thus Goldman's position can also be expressed as follows. The existence

2. Goldman, *A Theory of Human Action*, 10.

3. Kim, "Events as Property Exemplifications", 160-161. Kim's notation calls attention to the striking similarity between the Goldman-Kim identity conditions for events and the standard identity conditions for the ordered triples of set theory. Kim does in fact suggest that an account of events might for some purposes be developed along set theoretic lines (p. 161). He does not pursue this line; nor will I.

condition for events is that event $[x, P, t]$ exists if and only if the object x has the property P at time t; and the identity condition for events is that event $[x, P, t]$ = event $[y, R, t']$ if and only if $x=y$, $P=R$, and $t = t'$.[4]

Proceeding from his intuitions about the so-called by-relation, Goldman proceeds to spell out an account of how the acts in Davidson's examples are related, an account which is to avoid the ostensible problems which occur when the relationship is taken to be that of identity. To this end Goldman develops an account of a relation he calls "generation", which he means to encompass the relationships between acts supposedly expressed in phrases of the form "S did ⋯ by doing ---", "S did ⋯ in doing --- "[5] and stylistic variants of these employing phrases like "in virtue of", "by virtue of", "thereby", and possibly other prepositions.

This generation as conceived by Goldman is intended to be an asymmetric, irreflexive, and transitive relation. Furthermore, neither one of a pair of generationally related acts is "subsequent" to the other, where S's doing A' is subsequent to S's doing A if and only if it is correct to say that S did A and *later* did A'. This condition, that generationally related acts must be done during the same time, is a necessary, but not a sufficient condition for being generationally related.[6] Four kinds of not necessarily mutually exclusive act-generation are distinguished.

---

4. Although Goldman speaks mostly of acts or act-tokens because he is concerned with developing a theory of human action, the account is explicitly extended to include events which are not actions. See *A Theory of Human Action*, 3 n. 6, 44.

5. Goldman, *A Theory of Human Action*, 20, 38.

6. Goldman, *A Theory of Human Action*, 20-21. The possibility that this condition is not as straightforward as it appears to be will eventually be raised in the discussion below.

(1) Causal generation:

> ...*S*'s act-token *A* has a certain effect, *E*, and because it has this effect, *S* may be credited with performing act *A'*. For example, *S*'s flipping the switch has the effect of the light's going on. And in virtue of this, *S* may be credited with the act of turning on the light. That is, we may say that *S* exemplified the property of turning on the light. Similarly, *S*'s closing the door has the effect that a fly is unable to enter the house. Because of this, we may say that *S* exemplified the property of preventing a fly from entering the house. To generalize: *Act-token* A *of agent* S *causally generates act-token* A' *of agent* S *only if* (a) A *causes* E, *and* (b) A' *consists in* S's *causing* E.[7]

(2) Conventional generation:

In this type of generation "there is a rule, *R*, according to which *S*'s performance of *A* justifies the further ascription of *A'* to *S*." For example, suppose *S* extends his arm out the car window. Given the rule that extending one's arm out the car window while driving counts as signalling for a turn, *S*'s signalling for a turn has also occurred. Such examples may be expressed by the following condition:

> *Act-token* A *of agent* S *conventionally generates act-token* A' *of agent* S *only if the performance of* A *in circumstances* C *(possibly null), together with a rule* R *saying that* A *done in* C *counts as* A', *guarantees the performance of* A'.[8]

(3) Simple generation:

This differs from (1) and (2) in that there is no rule or causal relation involved. It is the (nonnull) circumstances in which *A* is

---

7. Goldman, *A Theory of Human Action*, 22-23.

8. Goldman, *A Theory of Human Action*, 25-26.

performed by S which ensure that S has performed A'. For example, if the circumstances are such that George has just jumped 6 feet then S's jumping 6 feet, 3 inches generates S's out jumping George. Mental states might also provide relevant circumstances for simple generation. For instance, if the circumstances are such that S is hoping to catch fish, S's dangling a line in the water generates S's fishing.[9]

(4) Augmentation generation:

A generates A' by augmentation if the description of A' is like the description of A but further modified (adverbially) as to manner or circumstance such that the former description entails the latter.[10] Thus for example S's running the mile, if done in the appropriate manner, will generate S's running the mile at 8 m.p.h.

Goldman suggests that the generationally related acts in particular examples can be represented diagrammatically by letting circles represent act-tokens and lines joining them represent the relation of generation; numerals can also be put on the lines to represent the kind of generation involved.[11] Thus Goldman might diagram Davidson's shooting-killing example in the following way:

9. Goldman, *A Theory of Human Action*, 26-27.

10. Cf. Goldman, *A Theory of Human Action*, 28. I have taken some liberties with Goldman's own characterization of augmentation generation in order to avoid use/mention confusion. Where he speaks of entailments between performances of acts, I speak of entailments between descriptions of acts.

11. Goldman, *A Theory of Human Action*, chapter 2, section 2.

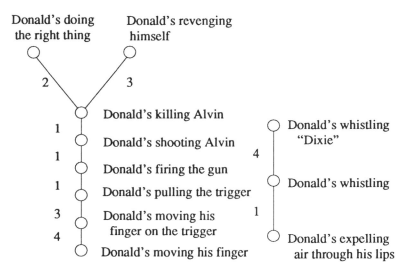

The branching might reflect the fact that Donald does the right thing by killing Alvin[12] and the fact that Donald revenges himself by killing Alvin, whereas Donald does not do the right thing by revenging himself,[13] nor does he revenge himself by doing the right thing.

A group of act-token nodes connected by lines of generation constitutes what Goldman calls an "act-tree". The separate tree on the right is a bit of embroidery on my part. It might indicate a set of generationally related acts simultaneous with but not generationally related to any of the acts in the shooting-killing sequence of the left tree—if we may suppose that Donald was cold-blooded enough to whistle "Dixie" while doing Alvin in!

12. Lest it be objected that this begs the question for or against certain views of rightness, let us stress the "convention" in conventional generation.

13. Assuming that there doesn't exist a code of honor, as in some Mediterranean cultures, which makes vengeance both a right and a duty.

Prima facie, this tree methodology seems to be a powerful tool for representing and explaining (via the generation relation) the sort of unity among actions that seems to be involved in Davidson's examples, without having to resort to identity claims and their attendant problems. A test of the superiority of this multiplying approach will be how it fares with respect to the problems raised by the three objections levelled against Davidson's unifying approach. This is what we will set out to determine in the next section.

For the record, let me also state now that what follows in the next section and beyond is not intended as an ad hominem defence of Davidson, but as a hopefully illuminating examination of the rival multiplying account. Davidson will be answered for in chapter 5.

3.2 Goldman and the Three Objections

We will now consider how satisfactorily the three problems for Davidson—which serve to partially motivate Goldman's account—can be handled or avoided by the multiplying theory.

First, let us take up the causal objection. Let us suppose for the sake of argument that Donald's pulling the trigger but not Donald's killing Alvin caused the gun to fire, which caused Alvin's death. Yet the trigger-pulling and the killing are not unrelated here. Recall the general principle for causal generation: act-token A of agent S causally generates act-token A' of agent S only if (a) A causes E and (b) A' consists in S's causing E. Interpreted for the case we are here considering, A will be Donald's pulling the trigger, E will be Alvin's death, and A' will be Donald's killing Alvin.

Does the trigger-pulling causally generate the killing? Clearly condition (a) of the principle for causal generation is met. What about condition (b)? If Goldman's particular paradigm examples for causal generation are to be accepted at face value we would have to say "yes". Trigger-pullings, shootings, and other actions which cause deaths are typically taken to generate killings.

But if the killing consists in the causing of Alvin's death, how does it differ from the trigger-pulling in that respect? Prima facie, Goldman appears to be committed to a position subscribed to by Davidson, viz. the position that "S's killing of R" is to be construed as "the action of S's that caused R's death".[14] If so, such commitment would support an identity between the killing and the trigger-pulling. If that, because of the causal objection, is a problem for Davidson, it is likewise one for Goldman. The issue here partly turns on how we read "consists in" in condition (b). Goldman does

---

14. Davidson, "The Individuation of Events", 229 <177>.

argue independently that "S's killing of R" does not mean the same as "the action of S's that caused R's death".[15] It is open for someone to argue that for this reason condition (b) is not met and that therefore Goldman is just mistaken about killings being causally generated by trigger-pullings. Such acts, the argument might continue, are in fact related by some other kind of generation.

To me such a move seems to undermine the raison d'être of causal generation. First, if sameness of meaning is required for "consisting in", one wonders how condition (b) for causal generation could ever be satisfied nontrivially. Secondly, since the objection to Davidson we are presently considering is after all a causal objection, one would expect the alternative account to address itself explicitly to the causal features of the situation. Causal generation, seemingly designed for just that purpose, is not adequate to it.

But let us take the suggestion up. What other kind of generation might be involved? It is clearly not conventional generation. Killing is not a matter of convention or rule the way signalling for a turn is. Augmentation generation is out since the requisite entailment is lacking. That leaves simple generation, which is also the most plausible. The circumstances in which A is performed by S which ensure that S has performed A' could include causal conditions. Unfortunately, Goldman claims that what differentiates simple generation from causal or conventional generation is that there is no rule or causal relation involved. Since Goldman takes the four kinds of generation to be exhaustive,[16] we can only conclude that something is amiss with his account in respect of the causal problem it was to avoid.

15. Goldman, "The Individuation of Action", 766, 768.

16. Goldman, *A Theory of Human Action*, 30.

Now we will see how Goldman fares with respect to the relational problem. It was claimed that when we speak of one act being done or performed by doing another, or alternatively in doing another, we are expressing the fact that a certain relationship obtains between these acts. This relationship is supposedly transitive, irreflexive, and asymmetric. The assumption of identity for acts so related seems to be at odds with this intuited relationship. Generation, we are to suppose, not only captures the relationship expressed in "by"- and "in"-locutions, but goes some way in elucidating its nature. Let us examine these contentions with respect to the following locutions:

(1) S signalled for a turn by raising his arm.

(2) In raising his arm, S signalled for a turn.

(3) In signalling for a turn, S raised his arm.

(4) S raised his arm by signalling for a turn.

It will be noted that (1) and (4) are converses of each other; likewise, (2) and (3). Since clearly none of (1)-(4) is solecistic, the by-relation cannot be held to be asymmetric because we "would not say" (in one sense of this phrase) one of a pair of mutually converse expressions but not the other. Goldman may have some other notion of irregularity in mind, but it would be counterproductive to speculate here what that might be.

Given that a statement expresses a certain relationship, a good indication (ceteris paribus) that the relationship in question is asymmetric is that the statement is true when its converse is false, or else false when its converse is true. Since irregularity is invoked to establish the falsity of the converse of a true "by"-locution, present concerns will best be served by addressing ourselves directly to the question of truth or falsity.

With this question in mind let us consider (2) and (3). Is there any reason why they could not both be said truly of one and the same pair of actions? In many contexts, whether one has said that S $verb_1$ed in $verb_2$ing instead of saying that S $verb_2$ed in $verb_1$ing seems not to matter as far as the truth or falsity of what one is saying is concerned. In such contexts, what differences there are can seemingly be explained as differences in emphasis. If the consideration cited in the previous paragraph goes towards showing that a relationship is asymmetric, then the existence of such contexts will for similar reasons go towards showing that a relationship is nonasymmetric.[17]

We note that (1) is nearly the same as (2), with "by" in place of "in", and that (4) is nearly the same as (3), with "by" in place of "in". If the difference between statements like (2) and (3) is not so great so as to yield asymmetry, it follows—if "by" and "in" express the same relationship—that (1) and (4) likewise do not express an asymmetric relation. Far from explaining an asymmetry, Goldman's view can be used to argue that there is no asymmetry to be explained.

Of course Goldman could just be mistaken in assimilating "by"-locutions and "in"-locutions as far as the relationships expressed are concerned. Work done by others suggests that this is so.[18] Since Goldman does on the whole tend to concentrate on "by"-locutions in

---

17. Beardsley, "Actions and Events: The Problem of Individuation", 276, suggests that the "in-relation" is nonasymmetrical. C.B. McCullagh, "The Individuation of Actions and Acts", *Australasian Journal of Philosophy* 54 (1976), 137, makes the stronger claim that the in-relation is always symmetrical.

18. E.g. J.L. Austin, *How to Do Things With Words*, ed. J.O. Urmson (New York: Oxford University Press, 1968), Lecture X.

his discussion, let us assume that the relationship in question is just that expressed by "by"-locutions and see where that assumption leads.

So we have a putatively asymmetric relationship expressed by "by"- (but not "in"-) locutions. How would generation help us to explain such a relationship? It might be thought that this is obvious, since the technical relation of generation is supposedly an extension and elaboration of the relationship intuited by Goldman as being expressed by the "by"-locution. I will show that this is far from obvious by indicating some serious difficulties that are engendered by the appeal to generation in explaining uses of the "by"-locution.

Let us turn our attention to these "by"-locutions again:

(1) S signalled for a turn by raising his arm.

(4) S raised his arm by signalling for a turn.

The question we are again raising is whether these can both be true in the same context. While they appear to have different senses and are not (straightforwardly) interchangeable in the way that the corresponding "in"-locutions might be, I see no reason why one must be false if the other is true. Certainly (1) and (4) are not formally inconsistent; nor do they seem jointly infelicitous on the face of it.[19] However, claims of possibilities are best supported by concrete examples. Let me proceed to provide a plausible one.

There is no problem as far as the generation of S's signalling for a turn by S's raising his arm is concerned. This is one of

---

19. Their conjunction certainly does not, for example, have the obvious infelicity of an assertion of the form "P, but I don't believe P".

Goldman's own paradigms of conventional generation. We can represent this by the diagram:

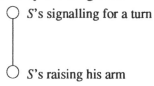

Now let us imagine the following scenario. A car is approaching a turn. On one side of the street is an indigenous person escorting a visitor from a backward country and untutored in the conventions of automobile driving. Wishing to instruct his companion in such matters, we might imagine the former pointing to the car, as it negotiates the turn with S's arm out the window, and saying something to the effect that by raising his arm, S is signalling for a turn. The preceding diagram captures this.

Further suppose that on the other side of the street are some secret agents of the RCMP, keeping tabs on S, who has infiltrated some subversive organization, two of whose members are with him in the car and watching his every move. The secret agents are too far from their own vehicle to tail the car. There is a secret button above the window which activates a homing device. The agents watch anxiously, since they know that S has to raise his arm without arousing suspicion in order to get his hand into the vicinity of the button. As the car enters the turn, the secret agents see the same sight that the visitor and his guide see. However, in this case the one agent remarks to the other that S raised his hand by signalling for a turn.

This appears to be a case of simple generation. S's signalling for a turn "consists in" his raising his hand under the circumstances. Had he used his flash-indicator, the desired act would not have been generated. This can be represented by:

○ *S*'s raising his arm

|

○ *S*'s signalling for a turn

Now we should be able to combine the two diagrams since the time involved in each is the same. We might try either of the following ways (there seems to be no basis for preferring one to the other):

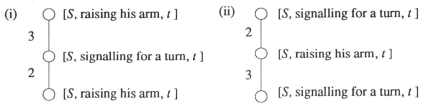

(i) ○ [*S*, raising his arm, *t*]

3

○ [*S*, signalling for a turn, *t*]

2

○ [*S*, raising his arm, *t*]

(ii) ○ [*S*, signalling for a turn, *t*]

2

○ [*S*, raising his arm, *t*]

3

○ [*S*, signalling for a turn, *t*]

In either case, something is amiss. For we seem to have generated act-tokens that in virtue of the asymmetry claimed for generation must necessarily be distinct. Yet in virtue of the identity condition the act-tokens represented by the first and third node on each tree are identical, since they involve the same agent, the same property, and the same time. So the notion of generation, or the criterion of identity (together with the existence condition for acts it presupposes), or both, must be defective. Furthermore, the particular defects are such that the purported asymmetry of the by-relation cannot even be intelligibly represented, never mind explained.

Has Goldman got any means of overcoming these difficulties? One move that has been suggested is that although in the one case the arm-raising generates the signalling and in the other case the signalling generates the arm-raising, this is not sufficient to undermine the alleged asymmetry of the generating relation because in each case there is a different kind of generating relation involved.[20] I do not think such a defence works.

On the one hand, the four kinds of generation are not assumed to be mutually exclusive.[21] On the other hand, an argument in defence of asymmetry which appeals to the kind of generation involved would also be an argument against the transitivity of generation when different kinds of generation are involved. This would effectively undermine the whole practice of putting acts generated by different kinds of generation on the same tree, and one would not be able to depict the unity among different acts which is suggested by Davidsonian examples and which must be accounted for if identities are to be denied. Thus it would seem that the raison d'être of the generational account requires that the different kinds of generation have a "core" in common.

In any event, whether or not the generation is of the same kind or of different kinds is irrelevant as far as the adequacy of the existence and identity conditions for actions is concerned. Only distinct acts are supposed to appear as nodes on an act-tree. The inescapable fact is that however the acts are generated, according to the criterion of identity there is still one node too many on each of the last two act-trees.

Goldman is not totally unaware that his existence condition for events is problematic, but he fails to draw out the consequences entailed for his theory. Goldman cites the case where someone points with his right hand and with his left hand simultaneously, thus being the agent of two simultaneous act-tokens of pointing.[22] He suggests this problem can be dealt with by specifying the way in which an

---

20. Put forth by R.X. Ware in conversation with the author.

21. Goldman, *A Theory of Human Action*, 30.

22. Goldman, "The Individuation of Action", 771.

act-token is performed. But such a move is not open to Goldman. After all, what is the relationship between pointing and pointing with one's hand? It is that of augmentation generation. Hence, specifying the way in which act-tokens are performed does not help to individuate them; it simply conjures up new act-tokens. Graphically the situation may be depicted thus:

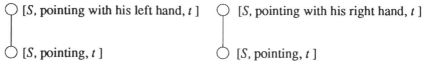

Thus, not only do we have two nodes for an act-token when by the identity criterion we ought only to have one, but in this case they are on different trees as well. We are forced to conclude that Goldman's property-exemplification account is no improvement over the identity thesis, when it comes to accommodating the by-relation.

Finally, we come to consider how Goldman's account would handle the temporal objection to the Davidsonian approach. Recall how the argument ran: Donald shoots Alvin at noon and since Alvin dies of the gunshot wound at midnight Donald kills Alvin and does so by shooting him; we would say that Alvin's death occurred twelve hours after he was shot, but we would not say Alvin's death occurred twelve hours after he was killed; therefore, the shooting is not identical with the killing.

If it is allowed that Donald's shooting Alvin generates Donald's killing Alvin at all, then it would appear that Goldman's theory is of no help in avoiding the temporal problem. *If* we would say it is the case, and it happens to be the case, that the shooting precedes the death by twelve hours, *then*, if the shooting generates the killing, the latter would occur at the same time as the former, and thus also precede the death by twelve hours whether we would say so or not. This is an immediate consequence of Goldman's requirement that generationally related acts are always done at the same time.

Of course Goldman is free to change his mind about shootings generating killings—and give up a paradigm!

Goldman does include in his account some consideration of actions which have temporal parts. An example he gives is the following:

> Consider, for example, S's act of driving a nail into the wall. Suppose this was accomplished by S striking the nail four times with a hammer.... There are four relevant basic acts performed during the period in question, at time t_1, t_2, t_3, and t_4 respectively. (Actually, each of these acts occurs over an interval of time, but for simplicity I shall speak as if each occurs at a moment of time.) Each of these basic acts is an act of S's swinging his hand, each of which generates an act of S's swinging the hammer, which in turn generates an act of driving the nail a little way into the wall. Thus, S's swinging his hand at t_1 generates S's swinging the hammer at t_1 which generates S's driving the nail a little way into the wall at t_1. The sequence of these four basic acts constitutes a larger act, viz., S's swinging his hand four times (between t_1 and t_4). This larger act generates S's act of swinging the hammer four times (between t_1 and t_4), which in turn generates S's act of driving the nail into the wall (between t_1 and t_4). None of the larger acts is generationally related to any of the smaller acts, but there are generational relationships among the three larger acts.[23]

A sympathetic question that might be asked, in the light of such an example, is whether, on a par with S's driving the nail (entirely) into the wall, the killing might be generated piecemeal by the shooting and subsequent acts, rather than holus-bolus by the shooting. That is, could such an account explain how Donald's killing Alvin, whilst beginning simultaneously with the shooting of Alvin, might

23. Goldman, *A Theory of Human Action*, 35-36.

continue after the shooting is over until the moment of Alvin's death occurs?

One does run a mile by first running half a mile, and one need not have run the entire mile to be running a mile. But the killing here is not quite analogous to running a mile. Once the shooting is over (we are supposing Donald fired just one death-causing shot) Donald need do nothing more to kill Alvin. It is not as if he is killing partly by shooting and partly by at a later time doing something else. After Donald shoots Alvin, all he has to do is wait for Alvin to die, but he certainly does not kill Alvin by waiting for him to die.

Perhaps some inaction on Donald's part, say letting Alvin die, or allowing nature to take its course, might do the trick. Those who oppose the "death with dignity" movement do, after all, claim that letting people die is tantamount to killing them.

However, that kind of move only works if it is available. We might suppose that Donald's shooting of Alvin is followed by in-stant remorse such that he does everything he can to prevent Alvin's death. Yet, if Alvin dies of the shooting, Donald will have killed Alvin nonetheless.

Lest it be thought that with enough ingenuity some property to carry the burden of generating the killing might yet be found—a property exemplified by Donald qua agent—even that possibility can be removed. Suppose that Donald's pulling of the trigger is immediately followed by his suffering a heart attack of which he dies instantly, while the victim, Alvin, as before, does not die until twelve hours later. If there is an act of killing performed by Donald it must have occurred no later than his shooting of Alvin. After that, Donald is only capable of exemplifying properties which don't re-quire his capacity as agent—such as the property of decomposing.

So it appears that Goldman's account is of no help with respect to the temporal problem either. The assumption that shootings generate killings in toto leaves Goldman with the same problem he accused Davidson of. An attempt to avoid this consequence by considering the killing in terms of temporal parts leads in certain cases to an inability to specify what generates the later parts of the killing.

Now it might be argued that my interpretation of Goldman's requirement that generationally related acts be done at the same time or during the same time is unduly strict and that I have in effect set up a straw man. I do not think this is so, but I am willing to entertain such a possibility. However, it will emerge that even a more "liberal" interpretation will leave the account with serious difficulties.

Here are Goldman's actual words with respect to the temporal restrictions on generationally related acts:

> ...neither one of a pair of generational acts is *subsequent* to the other. Let us say that S's doing A' is *subsequent* to S's doing A if and only if it is correct to say that S did A "*and then*" (or "*and later*") did A'....
>
> There is a sense, then, in which pairs of generational acts are always done *at the same time;* i.e., neither of a pair of generational acts is subsequent to the other....
>
> ...we do want [generational acts] to be performed at the same time—more precisely, during the same *interval* of time. The nonsubsequence requirement helps to ensure that they occupy the same interval of time. We must add to this, however, the requirement that no member of a...generational pair be a *temporal part,* i.e., proper part, of its...generational mate.[24]

Since the requirement that generational acts always be done at the same time is put in terms of mutual nonsubsequence there is room for another interpretation. If one act is not subsequent—in its entirety—to another, there is still the possibility that part of such an

24. Goldman, *A Theory of Human Action*, 21-22.

act might be subsequent to the other. This gives us a possible reading of the requirement which does not imply that the endpoints of generationally related acts be simultaneous. That is to say, that "during the same interval of time" does not mean "*throughout* the same interval of time".

Even if this less strict interpretation is what Goldman intended, it is not much of an advance since there are two immediate problems. The first is one which we have already mentioned in our discussion of temporal parts of killings under the strict interpretation. If the endpoints of the shooting and killing need not be simultaneous, we have namely the peculiar consequence that one could exemplify an act-property when one is not doing anything that can ordinarily be understood as performing an act.

The second difficulty of the less strict reading of Goldman's requirement is this. It would no longer be clear *which* "same interval" is in question when we speak of two generationally related acts occurring during the same interval of time. Relative to the act-tree they belong to, is it that of the act which occurs throughout the largest interval, or that having the smallest interval (a "basic act"?), or neither? Talk of "*the* same time" becomes mysterious. It cannot mean simply "a common time interval" since any two acts could trivially satisfy that requirement. At the very least more restrictions are needed and an explanation is owed.

Finally, even if we connived for the sake of argument with respect to these two difficulties, the suggested reading of Goldman's temporal requirement would create further difficulties for his existence condition and his criterion of identity.

Consider this example. Donald pulls the trigger and thereby shoots Alvin. His shooting Alvin causes grief to his mother, who fears he will be taken from her and jailed for his misdeed. At the hospital Alvin promises Donald's mother that he will tell the police the shooting was accidental, but just as Donald's mother is about to stop her grieving he unexpectedly dies of his wounds. The killing—which we will suppose has by now occurred—also causes her grief over the prospect of Donald's being taken from her, and her grief continues uninterrupted.

The tree for this story, where we will for simplicity's sake assume all the generations to be causal, will look like this:

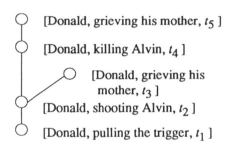

[Donald, grieving his mother, t_5]

[Donald, killing Alvin, t_4]

[Donald, grieving his mother, t_3]

[Donald, shooting Alvin, t_2]

[Donald, pulling the trigger, t_1]

If we suppose, as the suggestion goes, that the endpoints of generationally related acts need not be simultaneous then the times in the act-tokens could be related thus:[25]

$$t_1 \leq t_2 \leq t_3 \leq t_4 \leq t_5.$$

To address this supposition more specifically to the temporal objection, let us assume consistently with these temporal relations that the killing ends later than the shooting, i.e. that $t_2 \neq t_4$. To avoid unnecessary complication, let us also assume that $t = t_1 = t_2 = t_3$ and $t' =$

---

25. Strictly speaking, it is not the time intervals themselves that are related thus but the cardinal values associated with the respective intervals. I ignore this complication for convenience.

$t_4 = t_5$. Thus the time interval t' will include the time interval t. That is, t' will consist of t plus some other interval, say t^*.

Before proceeding, perhaps a word of explanation concerning the position of [Donald, grieving his mother, t_3] in the tree is needed. [Donald, grieving his mother, t_3] must appear on a separate branch for the following reason. On a Goldmanian account of the situation, while Donald grieves his mother (at t_3) by shooting Alvin (at t_2), he does not kill Alvin by grieving his mother (at t_3). However, Donald does kill Alvin(at t_4) by shooting him (at t_2). Thus the shooting generates the grieving and the shooting generates the killing, but the grieving does not generate the killing. If the grieving (at t_3) were not put on a different branch, either the transitivity of the generation relation would be violated, or else the requirement that no member of a generational pair be a temporal part of its generational mate would be violated—the latter because transitivity would make [Donald, grieving his mother, t_5] and [Donald, grieving his mother, t_3] a generationally related pair.

With the tree representation of the example thus sustained, the problem the example creates for Goldman is quite readily brought to the fore by the following observation. If Donald exemplifies *grieving his mother* throughout t', then he exemplifies that property throughout the parts of t', and hence throughout t. So if [Donald, grieving his mother, t'] is generated by the killing, its temporal part [Donald, grieving his mother, t] will ipso facto also exist. This picture results in conceptual chaos since we already have a node in which [Donald, grieving his mother, t] exists. That is, the generational property-exemplification account yields the existence of two distinct tokens of [Donald, grieving his mother, t] whereas by Goldman's existence condition and criterion of identity we ought only to have one.

There remains one possible move a multiplier might try in the face of this difficulty. He might claim that the grieving done during t in virtue of the shooting and the grieving done during t as subsumed under the grieving done during t' in virtue of the killing differentiate as to the way or manner in which they are done. As we saw in the discussion of the relational problem above where similar individuation difficulties arose independently of temporal considerations, such a reply will not work for a multiplier. Specifying way or manner merely creates additional act-tokens; it does not remove an unwanted one.

It has been demonstrated, then, that the suggested reinterpretation of the temporal restriction creates rather than solves problems for Goldman. We can conclude that the multiplying view either is itself vulnerable to the temporal objection, or avoids the temporal objection only at the cost of raising more serious difficulties for itself.

In conclusion, let me now summarize the results of this chapter. In the previous chapter I sketched three main objections against a Davidsonian unifying approach to event individuation, viz. the causal objection, the relational objection, and the temporal objection. Since multipliers take these three objections to motivate (partially) a multiplying account, one would have expected such an account itself to avoid the difficulties raised by these objections. I have argued and, I believe, established that such is not the case. With respect to the causal objection, it was seen that the multiplying account (at best) fared no better than Davidson's claims. With respect to the relational objection, it was seen that the multiplying account led to individuation difficulties. With respect to the temporal objection, it was seen that on a straightforward reading the multiplying account faced the same problem as Davidson, while on another plausible reading, led to individuation difficulties similar to those encountered with respect to the relational problem.

In the next chapter I will go on to examine some aspects of the multiplying account and its background assumptions with an eye for possible modifications which might avoid some of the more serious difficulties presented here.

4

A CONSIDERATION OF MODIFICATIONS
TO THE MULTIPLYING ACCOUNT

4.1 Preamble

At this point in the discussion, it is necessary to anticipate and fore-close a certain response which my documentation of the failure of Goldman's multiplying approach might provoke. The response in question involves the counterclaim that the problems I have raised for Goldman are problems for Goldman's account in letter only and do not penetrate to the underlying motivation and the outline of the theory. Since the difficulties are superficial, such a response might continue, the theory is susceptible to modifications which would avoid the problems I raised while leaving the theory substantially intact. That is, although Goldman's theory is faulty as stated, some close variant of it might nonetheless provide a correct account.

I am not prepared to argue that no modifications whatsoever would yield a correct account while retaining important affinities to the original. What I will do is show that although one sympathetic but critical way of reinterpreting Goldman enables us to get around some of the difficulties, it requires us to assume that a certain detail of Goldman's theory can be tampered with. This, I will go on to

LIBRARY OF DAVIDSON COLLEGE

suggest, cannot be done without also affecting features of Goldman's theory most central to it. Having thus answered the charge that the problems raised against Goldman are superficial, I will conclude by indicating a serious motivational problem the theory faces independently of whether or not it constitutes an adequate alternative to Davidson.

Before I begin, however, let me make an admission and a concession. Although I believe Goldman's theory incapable of satisfactorily handling the causal problem for the reasons that were adduced in the last chapter, I have no way of assessing the seriousness of this particular deficiency. Part of Goldman's problem here, it will be recalled, turned on the issue of how a key term ("consists in") in the conditions for causal generation was to be read. I am prepared to allow that this is a problem that can be remedied in some straightforward way without affecting the rest of Goldman's account—perhaps by specifying an intended technical sense for the otherwise misleading term. Hence, I will set Goldman's causal problem aside and make my case by addressing myself to the more serious individuation problems for Goldman's account encountered in the discussion of the relational and temporal problems.

4.2 An Example Retouched

Let us call back to mind the arm-raising/signalling case that was presented in the discussion of Goldman's account vis-à-vis the relational problem. There, against the backdrop of a certain story, and seemingly in accordance with Goldman's generational paradigms, we had an act-token of S's raising his arm generating an act-token of S's signalling for a turn, and also an act-token of S's signalling for a turn generating an act-token of S's raising his arm. This, as we saw, spelled disaster for the cotenability of Goldman's existence condition for events, his criterion of identity, and the asymmetry of his generation relation.

These last-mentioned tenets are basic to Goldman's multiplying account and would have to be among the items that remain invariant throughout modification, if we are to consider the results of modification as still being versions of *Goldman's* account at all. Modifications which directly violate any of these tenets are thus not deemed allowable modifications and will be excluded from consideration here.

The question now facing us is whether, within the constraints just indicated, Goldman's account can be modified to escape the unhappy consequences of the arm-raising/signalling case. I shall approach this question by way of a sympathetic reappraisal of the arm-raising/signalling case in order to isolate a troublesome feature of Goldman's theory as the most likely candidate for revision.

For me to tell a plausible story on Goldman's behalf with respect to the arm-raising/signalling case will require that I bring to the fore something merely implicit in my representation of Goldman's notion of generation thus far, but actually made explicit by Goldman in his most general characterization of generation.[1] What has to be made explicit is this: *establishing the occurrence of generation involves establishing the truth of a counterfactual claim. An act-token is generated by another act-token only if the situation is such that had the latter not occurred, neither would the former have occurred.*

Hence, in the case under reconsideration, the situation is as follows. S's raising his arm out the window generates S's signalling for a turn only if it is true that if S had not raised his arm out the window, he would not have signalled for a turn. Likewise, S's signalling for a turn generates S's raising his arm out the window only if it is true that if S had not signalled for a turn, S would not have raised his arm out the window (and thereby gotten his hand toward the hidden button).

So for such a case to involve Goldman in the difficulties indicated previously, it must be possible for the second counterfactual statement mentioned in the last paragraph to be true, given that the first one is (or conversely). Alternatively, for Goldman to escape the difficulties, it must be the case that the second counterfactual cannot be true, given that the first one is (or conversely).

I do not know how to establish such claims concerning counterfactuals in a satisfactory manner. If it is true that S might have gotten his hand toward the button in some way other than signalling, it is equally true that S could have signalled in some way other than extending his arm out the window, say by using his flash-indicator. Answers to such questions seem not to be an absolute matter but depend on what is built into the example. In *my* example, I would insist that if S had not signalled by doing what he did, he would not have generated the ultimately desired act-token.

---

1. Goldman, *A Theory of Human Action*, 33, 41ff.

For the sake of argument, however, I am going to grant Goldman the above-mentioned counterfactual claims that he needs. As well, I will connive with respect to some other counterfactual presuppositions needed to give Goldman as favorable a case as possible, provided these are not obviously unacceptable. Deciding what is favorable to Goldman and what he would be prepared to accept as acceptable is a vicarious undertaking and as such is subject to certain risks, not the least of which is that of misrepresentation. That can't be helped. The fact that the feature of Goldman's account that I isolate as a result of reappraising the arm-raising/signalling case is also one over which Goldman himself expresses reservations in a different context, does suggest, however, that my second-guessing of Goldman is not entirely off the mark.[2]

Now to specifics. The following diagram prima facie represents a more favorable alternative to the tree of generationally related act-tokens originally devised for the arm-raising/signalling case:

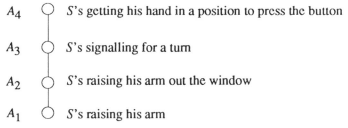

A_4 S's getting his hand in a position to press the button

A_3 S's signalling for a turn

A_2 S's raising his arm out the window

A_1 S's raising his arm

Here we manage to avoid the unhappy duplication of act-tokens we had in the original by what amounts to allowing Goldman suitable counterfactual presuppositions consistent with A_3's generating not another token of A_1 but instead something rather like A_4.

Let it be noted again that the counterfactual moves required to lend credence to such a picture would have to be quite involved.

2. Goldman's remarks will shortly be reproduced below.

Surely if we merely considered S's signalling as opposed to signalling by arm-raising or signalling by flipping the flash-indicator,
he need not have raised his arm (out the window). So just as we
might grant Goldman that it is not the case that had the signalling not
occurred the arm-raising would not have occurred, it also has to be
granted that there are good prima facie grounds for denying that had
the arm-raising not occurred the signalling would not have occurred.
For the sake of discussion, however, we are assuming this can in
principle be resolved. So in this case we are allowing Goldman both
the supposition that S would not have signalled had he not raised his
arm out the window and the supposition that the converse of this
does not hold.

Now notice what is implicit in the preceding proposal for the
generation of A_4. If anything is true of this case, it is surely that S
would not have gotten his hand in a position to press the button had
he not also raised his arm out the window *toward the button*. This
act-token (call it "A_5") of S's raising his arm out the window toward
the button satisfies the conditions for being related to A_4 by simple
generation. Furthermore A_2 satisfies the conditions for being related
to A_5 by augmentation generation. But where on the act-tree would
we put A_5?

Obviously it must be above A_2 and below A_4. But A_5 cannot be
placed between A_2 and A_3, since it is not true that had A_5 not occurred, A_3 would not have occurred—the propinquity of secret but-
tons to one's hand would not be encompassed in signalling conventions. But again A_5 would not have occurred had A_2 not occurred
(entailment points that way). So clearly A_2 must generate A_5 without
A_5's generating A_3. Perhaps in one of the following two ways:

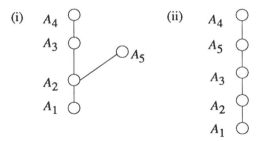

But how are we to express the generational link between A_5 and A_4. If we try to complete (i) by putting in lines to capture both the fact that A_4 was done by A_5 and the fact that if S had not signalled, he would not have been able to raise his arm out the window towards the button, i.e. that A_5 was done by A_3, we end up with a diagram that, if not unintelligible, is certainly without precedent in Goldman's account.

Diagram (ii) already represents the fact that A_5 was done by A_3; however, there does not appear to be a felicitous way of putting in a line to represent the augmentation generation of A_5 by A_2. This is a departure from what Goldman has led us to expect. This may not be a problem in one respect, since the transitivity of generation does guarantee that A_2 generates A_5 (although not by augmentation) and diagram (ii) does portray this. However, some remarks about why what appears to be a paradigm instance of augmentation generation cannot be represented as such should be forthcoming. At any rate, (ii) seems to be the best we can do with what's provided, and the generation relations represented therein do not violate Goldman's requirement that the generation relation be transitive, asymmetric, and irreflexive.

Thus, if we beg certain counterfactual questions and connive a bit with respect to augmentation generation, Goldman may have a way of escaping the consequences initially drawn from the arm-raising/signalling example. However, this sympathetic reinterpretation of the arm-raising/signalling example, in addition to requiring some slack for augmentation, also requires a departure from or reinterpretation of the evidence of the "by"-locution as it actually appears in discourse.

In the initial spelling out of the arm-raising/signalling scenario we had provided a context in which it could truly be said that S raised his arm by signalling for a turn (at t). Since Goldman subsumes the by-relation under his generation relation, we were thus able to claim that S's raising his arm was generated by S's signalling for a turn. The changes in counterfactual presuppositions in the current reappraisal of the example have not altered the fact that it can truly be said that S raised his arm by signalling for a turn.

In order to square this true "by"-locution with our current denial (on counterfactual grounds) that S's raising his arm is generated by S's signalling for a turn, we are compelled to take the event answering to "S raises his arm" as it appears in the "by"-locution as being different from S's exemplifying the property of raising his arm at t. Such a move implicitly acknowledges that the same action may be picked out under different descriptions after all.

This departure from the "by"-locutional evidence also suggests a motivational problem for Goldman. The relational objection against Davidson alleged that he failed to accommodate the "by"-locution. A motivation for the multiplying account was that it could succeed in accommodating this phenomenon as the generation relation. Since it does not, Davidson can justifiably level the charge of *tu quoque* against Goldman. Either Goldman has no case against Davidson in this respect, or he has a case which applies equally to his own account. Either way, an important motivation for Goldman's alternative to the identity thesis is lost.

4.3 An Example Untouched

Another individuation problem was attributed to Goldman in the last chapter. This problem was raised in both the discussion of the relational objection and that of the temporal objection, where we also entertained the suggestion that Goldman might escape his other individuation problems by specification of the manner in which acts were performed.

The problem, it will be recalled, was presented by a case where we had two seemingly distinct actions of S's pointing at t nonetheless coming out as identical on Goldman's criterion. Qualifying with respect to the manner of pointing was no solution since that only generated new acts by augmentation generation, as the diagrams here reproduced illustrate:

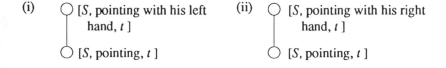

(i)   [S, pointing with his left hand, t]
       [S, pointing, t]

(ii)   [S, pointing with his right hand, t]
       [S, pointing, t]

This problem is different from the one we have been discussing so far in at least two respects. First, the offending duplicate act-tokens were generated on different trees, i.e. they were not related to one another by generation. Thus, unlike the situation with the previous problem, the asymmetry of generation is not directly a source of the difficulty.

Secondly, the statements which express the particular instances of generation involved here do not have natural or straightforward "by"-locutional correlates. Consider for example, the ring of "S pointed with his left hand by pointing" as compared with that of "S signalled for a turn by raising his arm". This would suggest that the difficulty here may lie with generation qua technical extension of the relation expressed by "by"-locutions.

One move that suggests itself as a possible way of avoiding the unwanted duplication of act-tokens here is that of denying that there is such an event at all as S's pointing (at t) simpliciter. That, however, would not do for Goldman. It would be tantamount to giving up a property exemplification account, since S surely does exemplify the property of pointing when he points with his left hand, say. That much is guaranteed by entailment.

Kim has pointed out that strictly read the existence condition for events does guarantee the existence of a unique event, [S, pointing, t], provided it is in fact true that S is pointing at t.[3] Since the latter can be true despite several simultaneous pointings by S, Kim would have it that likewise a unique event of S's pointing exists no matter how many pointings otherwise individuated by modification there might be.

Would such a claim be of help to Goldman here? In order to make use of it, it must be shown how the unique act of S's pointing, construed à la Kim, manages to generate (or is somehow in a "unity" with) both S's pointing with his left hand and S's pointing with his right hand. The following diagram might be proposed:

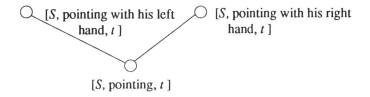

[S, pointing with his left hand, t]   [S, pointing with his right hand, t]

[S, pointing, t]

3. Kim, "Events as Property Exemplifications", 166.

This, however, does not seem quite right. If act-tokens on the same act-tree are supposedly somehow interdependent,[4] one might ask, what does pointing with one's left hand have to do with pointing with one's right hand? Indeed, Goldman himself would balk at such a representation, as it runs afoul of the distinction he makes in the following passage:

> Many pairs of acts done by a single agent at the same time are completely *independent* acts.... Suppose, for example, that S wiggles his toes while, at the same time, strumming a guitar. Neither of these acts is subsequent to the other, but they are not related by...generation. I shall call pairs of acts of this sort "*co-temporal*" acts. The criterion of co-temporality is the correctness of saying that one of the acts is done "*while also*" doing the other. It is correct to say that S wiggled his toes "while also" strumming a guitar; hence these two acts are co-temporal.[5]

It is difficult to see why S's pointing with his left hand at t and S's pointing with his right hand at t would not be independent acts of the same order as S's strumming a guitar and S's wiggling his toes.

Goldman does have another resource at his disposal which it was not necessary to introduce into the discussion so far, but which might be thought to have application here. Goldman introduces as a special case of augmentation generation a fifth kind of generation which he calls "compound generation".[6] In virtue of this compound generation act-trees can combine such that distinct and independent act-tokens may together generate what might be construed as a

---

4. Goldman, *A Theory of Human Action*, 21.

5. Goldman, *A Theory of Human Action*, 22. While I think that the correctness of being able to say one act is done while also doing another is inadequate as a criterion for independence, there is no point in getting sidetracked into that issue here.

6. Goldman, *A Theory of Human Action*, 28, 34ff.

"compound act". One of Goldman's examples[7] involving the jump-shot of basketball can be represented thus:

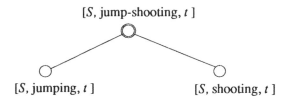

The node within a node is used to represent an act which may be generated in circumstances in which one act is done "while also" doing another. Thus the diagram reflects that the occurrence of S's shooting at t is a circumstance which enables S's jumping at t to generate S's jump-shooting at t, and vice versa, but avoids the infelicity of

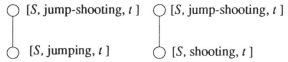

which suggests there are two tokens of S's jump-shooting at t. In addition "S's jump-shooting at t" has the force of and is interchangeable with "S's jumping *and* [or *while also*] shooting at t", since the property of jump-shooting is presumably the same property as shooting while jumping. Generally, independent but simultaneous acts can always generate a compound act denoted simply by conjoining the act-type expressions with "and" or "while also", whether or not there is in addition a standard label for such a compound act.

---

7. Goldman, *A Theory of Human Action*, 28.

Does this further notion of compound generation help vis-à-vis the original problem? It might now be thought that we can escape it by diagramming the situation in this way:

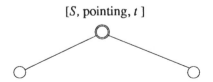

[S, pointing, t]

[S, pointing with his left hand, t]   [S, pointing with his right hand, t]

However this picture, given the counterfactual condition for generation (such as it is), conflicts with two counterfactuals which cannot reasonably be given up, viz. that S could have pointed at t even if he had not pointed with his right hand at t, and that S could have pointed at t even if he had not pointed with his left hand at t. Thus neither S's pointing with his right hand at t nor S's pointing with his left hand at t can generate S's pointing at t. However there is no similar problem attending the generation, from the two independent acts, of the compound act of S's pointing with his left hand while also pointing with his right hand. Hence we must conclude that the individuation problem cannot be sidestepped by invoking compound generation to generate a unique token of S's pointing at t either.

Finally, there remains one untried possibility that we may as well include here for the sake of completeness if not—in the light of what we've already seen—plausibility:

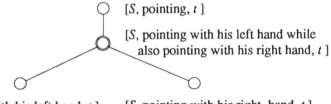

[S, pointing, t]

[S, pointing with his left hand while
  also pointing with his right hand, t]

[S, pointing with his left hand, t]   [S, pointing with his right hand, t]

where S's pointing at t is not itself gotten by compound generation but from a product of compound generation via some other kind of generation.

This alternative is precluded by reasoning similar to that of the paragraph before last. It is simply not true that S would not have pointed at t if S had not pointed with his right hand while also pointing with his left hand at t. Either hand would have sufficed. So this somewhat indirect appeal to compound generation is of no more help than the more direct one previously considered.

I cannot see any other apposite possibilities for representing the case under discussion within the confines of the generational machinery.

Let me state at this point the features of the foregoing reassessments that I wish to emphasize. Some limited gains were made on Goldman's behalf with respect to the arm-raising/signalling case, though this required (among other things) that some paradigms of augmentation generation not be treated as such. Unfortunately in the pointing case, where we started with a problem directly created by augmentation generation, similar success was not to be had. Nonetheless, these reassessments have yielded one major accomplishment in that they point to augmentation generation as source of difficulty. Thus in augmentation generation we have isolated a good candidate (ceteris paribus) for modification in Goldman's account.

Furthermore, there is a bonus of sorts. It will be recalled that Goldman's technical notion of generation is one abstracted from the phenomenon of the "by"-locution in everyday speech. However, with respect to augmentation generation Goldman himself remarks,

> The concept of augmentation generation, as I have characterized it, does not mesh completely with the other three forms of generation. And I think that, in general, it is not intuitively as attractive as these other species of generation. The feeling that it is rather different from the other three species is supported by the fact that the preposition "by" is inapplicable in connection with it. In all cases of causal, conventional, or simple generation it is appropriate to say that S did act A' "by" doing A. But we would not ordinarily say that S ran at 8 m.p.h. "by" running or that S extended his arm out the window "by" extending his arm. Nor would we say that S jump-shot (or "took a jump-shot") "by" shooting.[8]

Thus the feature we have isolated as a candidate for revision is one which Goldman himself considers anomalous and has misgivings about. Of course not too much should be inferred from this, but it does suggest that augmentation generation is the first thing Goldman would be prepared to give up, were he prepared to give up anything at all.

---

8. Goldman, *A Theory of Human Action*, 28-29.

4.4 Inclusion Excluded

So we have isolated in augmentation generation a feature of Goldman's theory which is the source of his individuation problems, ceteris paribus. Now we must consider the question of whether it is possible to modify the theory, within the constraints previously specified, by tampering with augmentation generation.

If we cannot have augmentation generation as it stands, what could we replace it with? Would it help the account, as one writer has suggested, to view acts related by augmentation generations as identical?[9] A moment's reflection will serve to verify that for Goldman the answer has to be "no". To return to our pointing case, *if* S's pointing with his left hand is identical with, rather than generated from, S's pointing, and likewise, S's pointing with his right hand is identical with, rather than generated by S's pointing, *then* by the principles of identity S's pointing with his left hand would be identical with S's pointing with his right hand—a patent absurdity! This absurd conclusion can only be avoided if we are willing to countenance distinct tokens of S's pointing at t, which is impossible given Goldman's criterion of identity. Therefore relinquishing augmentation generations in favor of identities would do little to take us beyond the original difficulties.

What are the alternatives to identity? Kim has suggested some form of "inclusion" in terms of which "such acts are different but

---

9. Beardsley, "Actions and Events: The Problem of Individuation", 276. Although I am criticizing Beardsley's proposal in the present context, I do not mean to suggest that, disengaged from Goldman's cause, the proposal would not otherwise be a perfectly sensible and indeed intuitive one. S's pointing with his left hand surely is a pointing of S's, if anything is. All I am claiming here is that Goldman cannot coherently make such seemingly straightforward identifications *within his account*, given its existence and identity conditions for acts and its generating relations.

not entirely distinct".[10] Kim's particular notion of inclusion, insofar as he says anything about it at all, turns out to be none other than Goldman's generation under an alias and is thus of no help in itself.[11] However the suggestion of inclusion in some other form might be worth pursuing.

Some of the intuitive appeal Kim finds for his notion of inclusion may derive from trading on associations with various notions of inclusion which have philosophical currency. Hence the possibility that one of these might be an improvement on augmentation generation merits consideration. In what follows, I will briefly take up some of these and give reasons why they won't do for Goldman's purposes.

Two forms of inclusion which have to be excluded at the outset involve the inclusion of spatial or temporal parts, as for example, running from 1st Street to 3rd Street might include running from 1st Street to 2nd Street, and running from daybreak to noon might include running from daybreak to mid-morning. The reason for excluding inclusion of these kinds should be self-evident; the inclusion, if such there be, of S's pointing in S's pointing with his left hand is not of this nature. If S is pointing and happens to be doing so with his left hand, little sense could be attached to the claim that S's pointing and S's pointing with his left hand occur in different places and over different time intervals.

Alternatively, the inclusion involved might be at one remove, viz. the inclusion of entailment: *that S* is pointing with his left hand entails *that S* is pointing. Even so, such inclusion in itself tells us more about meaning relations between terms (or relations among

10. Kim, "Events as Property Exemplifications", 170.

11. Kim, "Events as Property Exemplifications", n. 24; also see his "Noncausal Connections", *Noûs* 8 (1974), n. 3.

concepts) rather than about the things denoted by these terms (or the things falling under these concepts—although some philosophers are in the habit of speaking as if it established more.[12] Whether or not such inclusion is helpful or even germane depends on what one wishes to do with it—more pointedly, on what one assumes along with it. If one assumes that entailment relations between event descriptions mirror part-whole relationships between the events themselves, one is using the former as a criterion for the latter.

I believe such a criterion unsatisfactory for the purpose of picking out an intuitive inclusion relation to supplant augmentation generation. With respect to the case still under consideration, that S is pointing with his *right* hand also entails that S is pointing. Are we to conclude from such admittedly undeniable entailments that S's pointing with his right hand and S's pointing with his left hand have a part in common and so are not entirely distinct actions? That certainly does grate against the intuitions.

We can of course tell a special story to *make* such actions overlap, say, if S while pointing with left hand also uses it to support his paralyzed right hand in a pointing position. However, in the absence of such special circumstances, it is hard to imagine what sense could be attached to the claim that part of S's pointing with his left hand is included in S's pointing with his right hand. They are, ceteris paribus, entirely distinct actions.

Finally, we might consider the possibility of some kind of set theoretic inclusion involving the extensions of the act-properties exemplified. It is a common enough practice to speak of one property as being included in another, where this is meant to convey the fact

---

12. The connection between entailment and inclusion will be considered again in section 5.4. For the present my remarks are confined to the case of augmentation generation.

that the extension of one is a subset of the extension of the other. However, this kind of inclusion does not seem to be a likely candidate for lending weight to Kim's intuitions either. It is difficult to see how the fact that the extension of one act-*type* is included in that of another has any relevance at all as far as any *particular* act's being included in another is concerned.

However, even if it had relevance it would be of no use to Goldman since it would conflict with the main tenets of his account. His existence condition for events and his criterion of identity presuppose that every act-token is a token of exactly one act-type, and thus preclude the sort of inclusion just considered.[13]

The foregoing, I believe, exhaust the kinds of inclusion worthy of consideration as alternatives to augmentation generation—at least if "inclusion" is not to be a totally misleading word. At any rate, they are the only notions of inclusion I am acquainted with from the philosophical literature. While the preceding remarks on identity and the various notions of inclusion may not be the final word, they at least make manifest the difficulty of finding a replacement for augmentation generation within the confines of the multiplying account, and in the terms suggested by the literature in this area.

However, I think it is possible to make a stronger statement as to how things stand with respect to augmentation generation than the foregoing one. Inherent in any attempt to tamper with augmentation generation, the source of Goldman's problems, is the inability to confine such moves to just augmentation generation. That this is so is not difficult to demonstrate. For example, if S stabs Alvin, then, provided that S used the appropriate implement in the event, S's stabbing Alvin generates S's knifing Alvin by simple generation. But S's stabbing Alvin also generates, by augmentation, S's stab-

13. Goldman, *A Theory of Human Action*, 11.

bing Alvin with a knife. "*S* knifes Alvin" and "*S* stabs Alvin with a knife" mutually entail one another, for they are synonymous. Given the possibility of proceeding in such a fashion in so many cases, special moves against augmentation generation cannot be made which would not ipso facto affect the other kinds of generation as well. Augmentation generation overlaps and hence stands or falls with the other types of generation.

Considering the issue from a motivational point of view, there is another reason why the multiplying account can ill afford to dispense with augmentation generation. Generation as such was invoked by Goldman to provide an alternative account for a certain unity among events which were held to be identical by Davidson. Since generation had to be transitive to ensure this unity, it followed that the different kinds of generation had to have a core in common to ensure transitivity. Let us recall that early in this chapter just such a common denominator linking all the types of generation was emphasized, viz. that what is generated by what ultimately depends on the truth of certain counterfactuals.

If one were to give up augmentation generation, one would either have to give up the counterfactual basis for generation or adduce reasons why the counterfactual considerations should guarantee the occurrence of the other kinds of generation but not guarantee the occurrence of augmentation generation. The former would in effect deprive the account of both the rationale for its claims about particular cases and its explanatory force with respect to those cases. The latter, were it not already frustrated by the fact of generational overlap due to synonymy relations, would not be indicated by any save ad hoc considerations.

By now, I take it, it is obvious that the criticisms made against Goldman in the last chapter do not indicate mere problems in letter that are amenable to easy modification. Goldman's difficulties are deep-rooted and relatively intractable. We isolated in augmentation generation a feature of Goldman's theory as source of the problems and as candidate for revision. However, not only could we not find a suitable alternative to augmentation generation, but on closer examination it also became evident that augmentation generation was so intimately intertwined with the mainstays of the theory that it could not be tampered with without drastic consequences for the rest of the theory.

4.5 Counterfactuals Fingered

Throughout this chapter we have, in order to give Goldman a sympathetic hearing, in effect entered into collusion over certain counterfactual claims, and at a more general level, over the role of counterfactuals as such in his account. Before concluding this chapter, I think it apropos to register some suspicions concerning the latter. The fact that Goldman's multiplying account turns on counterfactuals at all, I will suggest, robs the account of its main motivation.

The concerns which prompted Goldman's account arose out of cases where Davidson would account for a certain unity among actions by holding actions differently described to be identical. This had odd-sounding or false-seeming results when substitutions into certain statements were made on the basis of the held identities. Such results, Goldman argued, invalidated the presumed identities.

Now let us consider, in outline, the Goldmanian approach with respect to such cases. Suppose, for example, that S moves his hand and that S frightens a fly and that these actions are so related that S frightens the fly by moving his hand. Davidson would account for the relatedness by suggesting that S's moving his hand and S's frightening the fly are the same event. Goldman, on the other hand, would account for this relatedness by taking the facts of the situation to materially imply that S's moving his hand *generates* S's frightening a fly. If we cash out the generation relation, this in turn entails that if S had not moved his hand, S would not have frightened the fly; or—in words better suited to our present purpose—that if S's moving his hand had not occurred, S's frightening the fly would not have occurred.[14] So Goldman has replaced the Davidsonian explanation of the unity of action in terms of identity with one in terms of counterfactuals.

However, counterfactuals do create an environment for singular terms in which obvious identicals cannot be truly or straightforwardly substituted. For example, we know as a matter of historical fact that

    (i) Nixon's succession to the presidency = Johnson's successor's succession to the presidency.

Furthermore, we know that

    (ii) If Humphrey had succeeded Johnson as president, Nixon's succession to the presidency would not have occurred.

However, if we substitute into (ii) on the basis of (i), we get

    (iii) If Humphrey had succeeded Johnson as president, Johnson's successor's succession to the presidency would not have occurred.

On the face of it, (iii) is either false or requires an unstraightforward reading—surely Johnson would have been succeeded by his successor no matter who won the election. However, it is not my purpose now to claim that (iii) must be false, or that contexts such as (ii) and (iii) must be opaque or oblique, or the like. My point is this. For an account which turns on counterfactuals to work, we must be able and willing to tell a special story about how the singular terms involved refer, in order to explain how false-seeming statements such as (iii) can be understood as consistent with identities such as (i).

14. Here I am taking the same liberties with singular terms that Goldman does. This will be addressed in section 5.3.

Without such an explanation Goldman's account is in certain respects on a par with Davidson's, for at some remove it would have similar oddities attending identity claims, as the preceding example shows. Since it was to such oddities that Goldman's account was originally addressed, no advance has been made. An additional worry is that Goldman's very criticisms of Davidson would be compromised, inasmuch as they are bolstered with counterfactual claims. These criticisms it will be recalled were what motivated Goldman's alternative multiplying account in the first place.

Even with such an explanation, however, Goldman would not be entirely off the hook as far as motivation for his own account is concerned. After all, the tactic of providing special explanations to square identity claims with the false-seeming statements they entail is just the sort of tactic Davidson could pursue too, in the face of Goldman's criticisms. (Conceivably the explanations could even turn out to be similar for both accounts.) So for his alternative account to be called for, what Goldman needs to provide as well is some reason for believing that this tactic wouldn't work in Davidson's case.

It is now evident that the multiplying account's counterfactual grounding constitutes a motivational embarrassment for Goldman. Our conclusion in this section—that Goldman's account is no advance over Davidson's account—restates and reinforces that of the last chapter. Moreover, it does so independently of the details of the account—the characterization of the types of generation, the criterion of identity, etc.—which were relied upon in that discussion. This makes the case against Goldman quite formidable and suggests that a reexamination of his case against Davidson is in order. That will be the task of the next chapter.

5

THE THREE OBJECTIONS RECONSIDERED

5.1 Preamble

So far, the evidence seems to indicate that neither the unifying nor the multiplying account fares too well with respect to the three problems which Goldman initially suggested were problems just for the former. However the last chapter makes it clear that this cannot be viewed as simply a choice between two views of equal merit, or demerit, as the case may be. Goldman's account fares the worse in that it is additionally plagued by severe and irremediable individuation problems. Furthermore, we noted a fundamental problem of motivation for Goldman which suggests, among other things, that he may have been too quick in his dismissal of Davidson.

However, to raise general doubts about Goldman's reasoning with respect to Davidson's identity claims is one thing. If we are to progress beyond such innuendo the following remains to be done. Sense must be made of the particular identity claims which are at stake. An understanding of the contexts within which the identity claims are made must be provided in order to satisfy whatever intuitions might prima facie be at odds with such claims. And finally, some indication of where the original reasoning went wrong must be given. To these ends, a reexamination of the original arguments brought to bear against Davidson will be the main undertaking of this chapter.

5.2 The Causal Objection

With respect to the particular example previously used to illustrate the causal objection to Davidson's so-called identity thesis, it will be recalled that we inferred

(4) Donald's pulling the trigger ≠ Donald's killing of Alvin

from the assumptions

(1) Donald's pulling the trigger caused the gun's firing

and

(2) It is not the case that Donald's killing Alvin caused the
     gun's firing,

where the inference appeared to be licensed by Davidson's own principle for event identity, viz. that events are identical just in case they have exactly the same causes and the same effects.

There is no point in seeking to invalidate this argument by attacking Davidson's principle for event identity. Although the principle is not without its problems as we will see in a later chapter, this particular argument does not stand or fall with Davidson's criterion. The usual principles of extensionality could serve in its stead.[1]

We turn then to the remaining alternative, namely, premise (2). As previously noted, the reasons Goldman would advance in support of premise (2) involve something to the effect that it would sound odd or counterintuitive to say that Donald's killing Alvin caused the gun's firing, or that we simply wouldn't say that this was so in the case envisaged .

Although, as I have previously indicated, what we would or would not say in certain circumstances is not always decisive,[2] in many circumstances acceptable inferences *from* what would or would not be said *to* what is the case can be readily made nonetheless. It is also not an unreasonable supposition, ceteris paribus, that the things we do say or would say carry somewhat more weight than the things we wouldn't say. For the example as presented, to say that Donald's killing Alvin did *not* cause the gun's firing *does* seem like a normal reaction. If we are to advance a Davidsonian position, we must determine why this is so and reconcile this fact with whatever sense we give to the identity claim in question.

It does not appear to be so for any immediately evident formal reason. The stress here is on "immediately evident". A formal reason, or the beginnings of one, might be found if one were to make explicit the times of Donald's killing of Alvin and of the gun's firing for the particular case at issue, and in addition had an analysis of causal relationships requiring the relata to be temporally ordered in certain ways. It is certainly not implausible that unexpressed beliefs

---

1. Cf. Goldman, "The Individuation of Action", 765. Here Goldman resorts to Davidson's principle in order to stress that "Davidson's treatment of particular cases of putative act identity founders on his own general criterion."

2. We recall that even Goldman's theory is forced to depart from such linguistic "facts" at some points.

regarding times might underlie the intuitions which seem to support premise (2), e.g. a belief that the killing could not have caused the gun's firing because the killing as such is not temporally prior to the gun's firing.

So viewed, however, the causal objection would turn in this particular case on the question of what time the killing occurred, which would in effect reduce it to the temporal objection. Since the temporal problem will be discussed again in its turn below we need not at this point address ourselves to this version of the causal objection.

If we are to get a handle on the causal objection in terms that are (prima facie) independent of the temporal worries, the present example again presents a problem. To do justice to the point at issue we must be able to decide to some extent what killings, as such, are. Davidson says, "To describe an event as a killing is to describe it as an event (here an action) that caused a death...."[3] If this contention is correct, then we would have an unproblematic way of understanding the claim that Donald's killing of Alvin caused the gun's firing, despite its perhaps inelegant or misleading wording. It does not seem to be objectionable that Donald's causing the death of Alvin have among its effects the gun's firing as well as Alvin's death. Indeed, in the example under consideration, for Donald to have caused the death of Alvin as he did, his action first had to cause the gun's firing.[4]

Now it might be thought that this way of giving sense to Davidson's claim is undermined by certain facts which, if Goldman

3. Davidson, "The Individuation of Events", 229 <177>.

4. Here I am making the assumption that some causal chains exhibit transitivity, which I do not think controversial. Whether causality as such is a transitive relation is another matter, but this is not the occasion for dealing with it.

and others are correct, would establish that expressions like "Donald's killing Alvin" do not mean the same as such causal counterparts as "Donald's causing the death of Alvin", "the action of Donald's which caused Alvin's death", and the like.[5] The reasoning here involves two contentions: first, that the facts cited demonstrate that "Donald's killing Alvin" does not mean the same as "Donald's causing Alvin's death"; secondly, that such difference in meaning shows that the expressions are not coreferential. In what follows, I will argue against both these claims.

The sorts of facts that are supposed to show that "Donald's killing Alvin" does not mean the same as "Donald's causing Alvin's death" are facts such as these: that one can cause the death of another by hiring, coercing, convincing someone else to kill him, that one can cause his death by letting him be killed by someone or something, and the like. Why do such facts establish the alleged difference in meaning? Because, we are told, getting or letting someone or something else to kill someone is not killing him. As Judith Jarvis Thomson says, "If I coerce Smith into killing Jones, then I cause Jones's death, but I do not kill him; Smith kills him."[6]

But it is not clear that such examples are true counterexamples to the meaning claims in question. Having killed by proxy is certainly not a defence against murder in a court of law. Also, we do say things such as, for example, that 6 000 000 Jews were killed by Hitler. It would be hard to convince the Israelis otherwise.[7] So it

---

5. Goldman, "The Individuation of Action", 765-766, 768. Also see Judith Jarvis Thomson, "The Time of a Killing", *Journal of Philosophy* 68 (1971), 122.

6. Thomson, "The Time of a Killing", 122.

7. If someone we presumed to be sensible said that Hitler did *not* kill 6 000 000 Jews, we would, in light of the public record on the Third Reich, regard such a person as either uninformed or quibbling over the estimate. Special contexts aside, it would take a Pickwickian frame of mind to regard such a person as correct for the reason

appears that having someone killed is killing at least in some contexts.

A response that might be made here is that such cases involve using the verb "kill" and its cognates in a special way.[8] Special or not, what is overlooked is that a parallel use exists for "cause" and its cognates.

Accusing someone of having killed constitutes "fighting words" in many circumstances—such accusations are often used in fixing direct responsibility, blame, or guilt. Hence we may not always say that S killed R when S caused R's death at several removes, because the responsibility etc. may not be as great or may be more diffused at that remove, or because attributing responsibility might for some reason even be inappropriate at that level. However, it is plain that we are often equally reluctant to single out someone as having caused a death in such contexts. When we don't want to put the entire responsibility or blame on some agent at several removes down the causal chain, we often mitigate our remarks by speaking in terms of "*indirectly* causing" as opposed to causing, by speaking of contributing factors, or by seemingly denying causal agency altogether. We might say, for example, "Of course S did not cause R's death, but had he not done what he did, R's death might not have occurred," and be perfectly well understood.

Granted, this too may involve a special use of causal idioms. The point is that they can be paired with the purported special uses of "kill" in such a way that the type of sameness of meaning in

---

quoted from Thomson. And that's why it does not even occur to us that Ernst Zundel might be philosophically astute instead of just plain nutty.

8. Judith Jarvis Thomson, *Acts and Other Events* (Ithaca, N.Y.: Cornell University Press, 1977), 128 n.1.

question need not be given up. To respond to Thomson's remark, if I cause Jones's death by coercing Smith into killing him, it may be true that in some (unspecified) sense I have not killed Smith. But in that sense perhaps I haven't caused his death either.

Clearly, then, more is needed to show that expressions of the form "*S*'s killing of *R*" and "*S*'s causing *R*'s death" are not the same in meaning. However, even if that can be established by means of other considerations, still more is needed to show that such expressions do not denote or refer to the same event. All that differences in meaning of the kind Goldman and Thomson have argued for would establish is that not all causings-to-die are killings. It does not rule out the converse, that all killings are causings-to-die, much less the weaker condition that some actions are both killings and causings-to-die. So it appears that our way of making sense of Davidson's identity claim has not been invalidated by the response we have been considering.

We have, then, indicated how we might understand Davidson's identity claim and have found grounds for rejecting certain moves intended to count against that way of understanding it. It still remains, however, to account for the fact that it does seem to be a normal reaction to say of the example as presented that Donald's killing Alvin did not cause the gun's firing. How is that fact to be reconciled with Davidson's identity claim which in the context under discussion forces the conclusion that it is the case that Donald's killing Alvin caused the gun's firing? What rationale could there be for holding that conclusion to be merely awkward or misleading, say, as opposed to false? I will now proceed to provide answers to these questions.

The widely held view that explanation contexts are nonextensional suggests a way of resolving the above discrepancy.[9] I will endorse that view without argument. Another widely held view maintains that verbal specifications of causes are causal explanations.[10] I do not agree with this view on its strictest reading. However, I will endorse and partially defend a qualified version of this view. I will hold that verbal specifications of causes are *commonly* causal explanations. It follows immediately from these assumptions that verbal specifications of causes commonly provide nonextensional contexts. This, together with other considerations, will enable us to defuse arguments based on the apparent failure of identity substitutions in certain verbal specifications of cause.

While I do not pretend to have an account of causal explanation up my sleeve, this much seems safe to say: Many unarguably exemplary causal explanations, while about particular events, nevertheless somehow describe or typify them such that in general events of the sort typified in one way are regularly followed by events of the sort typified in another way. Thus, when a particular specification of cause and effect is given, its explanatory force *often* derives from and is sensitive to the choice of words.

9. See for example Beardsley, "Actions and Events: The Problem of Individuation", 273; Fred I. Dretske, "Referring to Events", in *Studies in the Philosophy of Language*, Midwest Studies in Philosophy, vol.2 (Morris, Minnesota: University of Minnesota Press, 1977), 94; and Israel Scheffler, *The Anatomy of Inquiry* (New York: Alfred A. Knopf, 1969), 66-68.

10. See for example Beardsley, "Actions and Events: The Problem of Individuation", 272; Mario Bunge, *Causality* (Cambridge, Massachusetts: Harvard University Press, 1959), 298-299; Carl G. Hempel, *Aspects of Scientific Explanation and Other Essays in the Philosophy of Science* (New York: The Free Press, 1965), 347ff.; and Michael Kubara, "Strictly Speaking and Other Actions" (Commentary on Karl Pfeifer, "Time, Death and Event Identity" read at the Annual Meeting of the Canadian Philosophical Association, University of Saskatchewan, June 4, 1979), 3.

The foregoing remark on regularity is of course an oversimplification, and the point about sensitivity, too, has to be qualified to accommodate vagaries of context. Consider for example, the following typical specification of cause:

(a) The ringing of the alarm caused John to awaken.

This specification might be deemed explanatory with respect to why John awoke because ringing alarm clocks are just the sorts of things that generally might be expected to awaken people. The words employed in the event-describing expressions embedded in (a) openly hint at such a correlation—or "lawlike connection", as some would call it. In the case of (a), then, a common awareness of a *fair* correlation between two types of events lets (a) work as a causal explanation. The word "fair" emphasizes the oversimplification regarding regularity. That the superficial generalization which corresponds to (a) must be true if (a) itself is to be deemed explanatory and/or true would be too much to expect. The notion of regularity that is at issue is not that of strict correlation but one that is indicated by the presumption of inhibiting factors when correlation fails.

Considerations of causal regularity, I suspect, will account for its being a natural reaction, as Goldman maintains, for saying of the Davidsonian example that Donald's killing Alvin did not cause the gun's firing. However, such an accounting would seem to provide the opposition with yet another rejoinder.

The countermove is this. The connection between causal specification and causal explanation is so intimate, it could be claimed, that a statement cannot succeed as a specification of cause and effect unless it functions as an explanation as well.[11] So the statement at issue, viz. that Donald's killing Alvin caused the gun's firing, does not merely *seem* false, as defenders of Davidson might claim. In virtue of this intimate connection it simply *is* false. It cannot be understood as both a true and a cause-specifying statement.

Given the way that causal explanation has been characterized in terms of regularity above, it would appear that such a move excludes too much. Consider for example another typical causal statement:

(b) The outbreak of World War II caused the British fascist movement to wither away.

Clearly in this specification of cause and effect there is no hint of regularity on a par with that to be found in (a) above. One would be hard pressed to find correlations between outbreaks of war and fascist decline, let alone wars of the global variety and decline of fascism in its Anglo-Saxon mode.

However, let me play Devil's advocate for the moment and sketch an argument on behalf of the opposition. I will contend that this reply is too facile in that it meets the letter rather than the spirit of the claim it is advanced against. Despite the prima facie differences between (a) and (b), I will suggest how a plausible case might be made for assimilating statements of the kind exhibited by (b) to the kind exhibited by (a).

Statement (b) is a statement of historical dimensions in a way that (a) is not. The very singular terms in it already figure as complex and abstractive summations of more mundane occurrences, and

11. This countermove amounts to endorsing the strict version of the view that verbal specification of cause are causal explanations, which I eschewed above. By arguing against this view I will be indirectly defending the weaker stance I myself endorsed.

for (b) to work as a statement at all one must have some idea of what counts as the outbreak of W.W. II and what counts as the decline of British fascism. This suggests that statements like (b) are best approached by way of considering what sort of pursuit anyone making them would be engaging in.

When historians, whether of the classroom or the barroom, make statements like (b), the presumed rationale or methodology of their pursuit may already commit them to the assumption that there is something about the outbreak of W.W. II and something about the demise of British fascism which is an instance of a regularity. Such indeed has been argued elsewhere.[12]

If this view is correct, it would appear that although these events are not described in a manner that displays a regularity, they can nonetheless be so described in principle. Furthermore, statements like (b) do not occur in vacuums, but against backdrops of known facts, beliefs, assumptions, etc., which are often merely implicit. So it may well be that it is the backdrop rather than the explicit expression which carries the burden of the explanatory force for statements like (b).

Another way of putting the point is this. While the causal relationship is not explicitly specified in terms from which a regularity can be read off, an adequate analysis of (b) in context would have to be in such terms. W.W. II has to be understood as causing what it does qua some characteristic it has, and likewise the decline of fascism in Britain as an effect has to be understood qua some characteristic it has. Otherwise (b) would be somehow wanting as a causal specification. Similarly, of course, in the case of (a), the ringing of

---

12. E.g. Morton White, *Foundations of Historical Knowledge* (New York: Harper and Row, 1965), chapters 2 and 3.

the alarm clock has to be understood qua its ringing, but this qualification would normally be redundant in such specifications.[13]

I have suggested that in the case of (b) it is the backdrop, not the verbal specification, which carries the burden of the explanation. However, it is clear that this feature only superficially differentiates type (b) from type (a). It is a consequence of biology and culture that certain regularities are entrenched in our ways of thinking and that certain verbal specifications suffice as explanations in the barest of contexts. A Martian on the other hand might have to be told something about the purpose of alarm clocks and what it is about their ringing that interrupts human sleep if (a) is to work as an explanation for him.

Hence the previous suggestion that the point about an explanation's sensitivity to word choice needed qualification comes to this: what words enable a specification to work as an explanation is to a large extent dependent on when and where and who is explaining what to whom. Put more bluntly, the difference between (a) and (b) can be cashed out as a difference in degree. So statements like (b) can be assimilated to statements like (a) on some story, with their intuitive difference coming to no more than one of relying on context to a different degree. This establishes that where regularities are not openly apparent in the verbal specification of cause, singular causal statements may nonetheless still work as explanations. Furthermore, at the level of abstraction suggested by (b) it may well be that a case can be made that one cannot really apprehend the intended causal relationship unless the specification thereof already constitutes an explanation.

---

13. Goldman would perhaps argue that the redundancy is a necessary one, since for him the ringing of the alarm clock is none other than the alarm clock's exemplifying the property of ringing.

The preceding remarks suggest that Goldman et al. would have a strong case against Davidson in the claim that there is no causal specification without causal explanation. But what these remarks also suggest is that we have been looking for counterexamples to that claim in the wrong places. Causal specifications in history may already be skewed, given the nature of the historical enterprise. The same probably holds for pursuits involving similar levels of sophistication and abstraction. Let us turn, then, to an example involving cruder appreciation of causal relationships.

Accounts or fictionalizations of contacts between advanced and primitive cultures provide a rich source of such examples.[14] Consider the savage who is told to point and pull what to us are respectively a gun and its trigger. For the savage there are two unusual events, viz. his pulling a thing sticking out from a strange object and the immediately ensuing recoil, crashing sound, puff of smoke, and appearance of a large hole in the object pointed at. What sort of causal specification could the savage give his fellow tribesmen? "I pulled this thing on it and that made it do that" probably would capture it. Has the savage apprehended the causal connection between the two novel events? His throwing the gun away and running for cover, or his quick offer of cattle and wives in exchange would be evidence that he had. Has his causal specification, such as it is, succeeded in making manifest the causal relationship to his fellow tribesmen? If they too are lining up with offers of cattle and wives he would seem to have gotten the message across. That much is supported by a well-known causal connection—that between perceiving something as an advantage and wanting it.

There is no good reason, it appears, for denying that our savage has succeeded in making and communicating a true causal statement.

14. Not to mention C.B. Martin, who drew my attention to such examples.

But his statement does not allude to any regularities explicitly and there certainly aren't any that he and his tribesmen could be implicitly aware of, given their hypothesized ignorance of firearms technology. They have no fair correlations between pulling little levers on strange objects and loud noises, smoke, and holes to fall back on that would explain how and why the former caused the latter.

Here, then, we have a counterexample to the thesis that there cannot be causal specification without causal explanation. There may of course reside in causal specification a commitment to the existence of some explanatory regularity or other, but that is another matter and does not vitiate the point.

Now I think we are in a position to venture an explanation of both why it seems natural enough to deny that Donald's killing of Alvin caused the gun to fire and why that is not a problem for Davidson's identity claim and its consequences. Suppose

(i) Donald's killing Alvin caused the gun's firing

is the result of substituting the identity

(ii) Donald's killing Alvin = Donald's pulling the trigger

into

(iii) Donald's pulling of the trigger caused the gun's firing.

If (iii) provides an explanation context, then naturally something can be expected to go wrong with (i) in the role of (iii). It is, after all, qua trigger-pulling and not qua killing that Donald's action causes the gun's firing. If the assertibility conditions in ordinary circumstances ensure that a statement like (i) has the force of, say,

(iv) Donald's action qua killing of Alvin caused the gun's
firing,

then for such contexts there would be every reason to take (i) to be
false, as Goldman wants it, rather than merely odd.

This point can be reinforced if one notes a peculiar feature of (i)
which makes it inherently unsuited for the role of causal explanation
as conceived above. The verbal specification of the action which
caused the gun's firing *as a killing* makes use of a characteristic the
action could only have in virtue of an effect it happens to bring
about—in this case, Alvin's death. Such a specification of Donald's
action could hardly be explanatory of Alvin's death or of any inter-
mediary events in the causal chain leading to Alvin's death, such as
the gun's firing. Unlike the above historical causal statement (b),
which at least promises explanation relative to a backdrop, such a
specification as (i) actually confounds the explanatory role that is
commonly expected of a causal specification.

The fact that a verbal specification of cause for a certain kind of
example not only is not, but *could not* be explanatory as far as certain effects' taking place is concerned accounts in a fully general
way for the presumed falseness of specifications like (i). Hence
such presumptions are not to be written off as merely unfortunate
intuitions about underdetermined artificial examples.

However, by now it should be clear that they no longer have to
be written off as far as the unifying position is concerned. If (i) does
provide an explanation context, as I have argued on behalf of causal
claims ordinarily made, then I think the tendency to count (i) as
false, when assumed to be of the same ilk, might be justifiable. But
what follows from this? Not, I suggest, that Davidson's claim is
mistaken as such, but that his claim would be mistaken *if* his verbal

specifications of cause were specifications-cum-explanations in the ordinary way. That there can be verbal specifications of cause which are not explanations has already been established; so the argument against Davidson can proceed only if it can show the protasis to be somehow a consequence of the unifying position. As far as I can determine there is no reason to regard Davidson as being committed to such a position. He can simply deny that when he expresses a causal claim à la (i) he means it to be understood as (iv), notwithstanding the fact that in daily discourse it might nevertheless be so taken. He can argue that the assertibility conditions for an expression like (i) are, within the context of a philosophical theory such as his, different from those of normal pragmatic contexts.

Thus we see that the causal objection, despite its initial impact, does not cause problems that cannot be handled by a Davidsonian unifying position. I suspect that much of the initial force this objection has derives from the particular nature of the shooting-killing example.[15] Other examples generally are not nearly so convincing. Consider this one Goldman also provides:

> Suppose that John is playing the piano, and that his playing causes Smith to fall asleep while also causing Brown, who was already asleep, to wake up. John has performed the following acts: (1) he has played the piano, (2) he has put Smith to sleep, and (3) he has awakened Brown. According to the identity thesis, John's playing the piano = John's putting Smith to sleep = John's awakening Brown. But are these genuine identities? Consider the following two events: (e_1) Smith's falling asleep and (e_2) Brown's waking up. *Ex hypothesi*, both of these events were caused by John's playing the piano. Now let us compare John's playing the piano with John's awakening Brown. Clearly, while John's playing the piano caused (e_1), Smith's falling asleep, John's awakening Brown

---

15. The verb "kill" is a particularly troublesome verb to begin with, if the number of articles linguists have devoted to it alone is any indication. See the bibliographical entries for Kac, Shibatani, and McCawley.

did *not* cause (e_1). Similarly, compare John's playing the piano with John's putting Smith to sleep. John's playing the piano *did* cause (e_2), Brown's waking up, while John's putting Smith to sleep did *not* cause (e_2). We see, then, that John's act of playing the piano has a property which is lacked by John's act of putting Smith to sleep and has another property which is lacked by John's act of awakening Brown. Hence, John's playing the piano cannot be identical with John's putting Smith to sleep and cannot be identical with John's awakening Brown.[16]

Here, Goldman's denial that John's putting Smith to sleep caused Brown's waking up does not seem to have nearly the clout that attached to his denial of the crucial premise in the shooting-killing case.

Is it mistaken to say that John's putting Smith to sleep caused Brown to awaken? There seems to be no inherent reason why the act of putting one person to sleep cannot cause another person to awaken. Perhaps if one were unaware of the circumstances, one's curiosity might be whetted by such a statement. But that would go no farther towards establishing such a claim to be false than the fact that someone ignorant of 20th century history might be puzzled by the claim that the onset of W.W. II caused British fascism to wither, would go towards showing that the onset of W.W. II did not cause British fascism to wither. All that follows is that the form of words does not make the lawlike connection manifest.

Here in fact it does seem plausible to say that John's putting Smith to sleep caused Brown to awaken, because John did put Smith to sleep *with piano music* within Brown's earshot. Put another way, there are other descriptions available for designating John's putting Smith to sleep—e.g. "John's putting Smith to sleep with piano music"—which more openly suggest the appropriate

---

16. Goldman, *A Theory of Human Action* , 2-3.

lawlike connection and thereby make the causal claim less puzzling.[17]

This concludes my reconsideration of the causal objection to Davidson.

17. This point appears in Norvin Richards, "*E Pluribus Unum:* A Defence of Davidson's Individuation of Action", Philosophical Studies 29 (1976), 194. Goldman would of course not countenance such redescription of events, since different properties are ascribed. However, that stance and the theory that comes with it were initially motivated by the intuited falseness of causal claims like the claim in question, and thus cannot be used in support of such intuitions.

5.3 The Relational Objection

Next, we will reassess the relational objection to Davidson's identity thesis. For the particular example used to illustrate this objection, it will be recalled that from the premises

(1) John turned on the light by flipping the switch

(2) It is not the case that John flipped the switch by turning on the light

(3) It is not the case that John turned on the light by turning on the light

it was to be inferred that

(4) John's flipping the switch ≠ John's turning on the light.

The reasoning Goldman claimed to be employing here was as follows. There is a relationship predicated of two acts in (1) which, witness (2), must be asymmetric, and witness (3), must be irreflexive. Identity is both symmetric and reflexive. So the relationship in question cannot be one between identicals.

Before providing my own criticisms of this argument, I shall first undertake to defend it against what I believe to be a wrongheaded objection.

The objection in question is one that has been raised by Judith Jarvis Thomson.[18] Her point is that the apparent logical structure of this type of argument does not permit the purported reasoning to go

18. Judith Jarvis Thomson, "Individuating Actions", *Journal of Philosophy* 68 (1971), 775ff.

through. The alleged problem is that none of the premises contain the singular terms for acts found in the conclusion, viz. "John's flipping the switch" and "John's turning on the light". Clearly these or somesuch implicitly coreferential with these will be required at some level of analysis, if the argument is to succeed.

Enough slack might be allowed to regard the string "flipping the switch", which appears in (1) and (3), as in these contexts elliptical for something like "John's flipping the switch" or "his flipping the switch", the latter perhaps being preferable in that it could be more felicitously incorporated into the sentences in question. The corresponding move could be made for "turning on the light" in (2).

I do not see anything objectionable in allowing that there is such slackness. However, even if these accommodations are made, there will still not be enough singular terms in the premises, as they stand, to permit Goldman's line of reasoning about *relations*.

Thomson makes the suggestion that perhaps Goldman thinks his "by"-locutions are analyzable or paraphrasable into something that does contain the singular terms required to give the argument a valid form. Barely having proposed this, however, Thomson goes on to argue against the possibility of such a paraphrase. Here are her remarks:

Goldman says of Miss Anscombe's man that

(2) He replenished the water supply by operating the pump.

... So perhaps he thinks (2) is paraphrasable into

(2') His replenishing of the water supply has the by-relation to his operating of the pump.

and that it is into this that we are to make substitutions by appeal to (1).

But *is* (2) paraphrasable into (2')? Suppose Miss Anscombe's man has been pumping away every morning for weeks; only today, for the first time were the pipes in order, and so only today, for the first time, did he replenish the water supply by operating the pump. Then (2) is true. But if in saying (2') the replenishing I refer to is today's and the pumping I refer to is yesterday's, then—in light of what one supposes Goldman means by 'the by-relation'—(2') should be false. The difficulty here... [is that] 'He verbed' doesn't itself contain any expression referring to a particular act, and is true even if he verbed many times, whereas the nominalization 'his verbing' constructed from it purports to refer to a particular act.[19]

I have three comments in response to Thomson on this point. First, let me speak to the insinuation that a sentence containing no singular terms for acts cannot purport to pertain to a particular act, as can the nominalizations constructed from such sentences. Such a contention is clearly false. Suppose a prankster makes the report "Sam fell in the lake" at a time when Sam has not recently been anywhere near the lake. The fortuitous fact that Sam had fallen in the lake three years previously would not let the prankster off the hook—he was not reporting ancient history. His statement only works as a prank because it purports to report a particular recent event, which as it happens did not occur.

Consider also a situation where equivocation is resolved:

A: Sam fell in the lake again. He nearly drowned.

B: I was there. But to me it looked like he was just fooling around.

A: That was yesterday. I'm talking about this morning.

---

19. Thomson, "Individuating Actions", 775.

That such clarification is at all appropriate points to the fact that expressions such as "Sam fell in the lake" commonly purport to be about, and are taken as purporting to be about, particular events.

My second comment is in respect of a possible objection that might be raised against my first comment. It might be protested that what I have said about statements pertaining to particular events is a question of pragmatics, not logical form; thus it is irrelevant as far as the question of the validity of Goldman's argument is concerned.

Here I would insist that we cannot begin to determine logical form without first making certain pragmatic assumptions. Expressions *per se* don't refer unless they are employed to that end. Therefore, the difficulty Thomson has with Goldman's "by"-locutions should also be a difficulty for any occurrences of singular terms in an argument. By the form alone we have no guarantee that "John" refers to the same person from one line to the next in the argument above; nor would there be any guarantee that "he" in Thomson's (2) has the same antecedent as "his" in her (2'). "John *verb*ed" may be true even if many Johns *verb*ed—or if many did not, for that matter.

So unless there is something I have missed, Thomson seems to be demanding more of sentences vis-à-vis their nominalizations than would ordinarily be demanded of names vis-à-vis their replicas. When it comes to paraphrasing arguments, charity requires, ceteris paribus, that equivocality arising from the generic nature of language be resolved in a manner that allows the arguments to work.

Thirdly, even if there is something I have missed and Thomson does have it right that Goldman's premises cannot be suitably paraphrased, this would not in itself invalidate the argument. Conditions which are merely sufficient for the truth of the premises but which exhibit the appropriate logical form might be stated. Then Goldman's argument would be valid, provided the parallel (but not quite paraphrastic) argument having the stated truth conditions as premises is valid.

I will eventually have recourse to such reasoning below. For present purposes, though, we need not go to such lengths. As it happens, the objection about singular terms can be met in a simpler and more direct manner.

Fortunately there is a way of looking at the current matter by virtue of which worries over Goldman's self-styled relational reasoning, and the logical structure required for that reasoning to be applicable, turn out to be a red herring as far as the argument is concerned.

What no one seems to have noticed about Goldman's argument is this. The gist of the argument can be captured without relying on the notion of a by-relation and without the need for paraphrase of a major sort. All that's needed is the slackness spoken of earlier, premises aptly chosen from those available, and a bit of judicious regimentation. The argument will then be seen to have the sort of structure that permits the conclusion to drop out by the usual rules of extensionality.

The procedure is as follows. First we take premise (1) and regarding "flipping the switch" as elliptical for "his flipping the switch", parenthesize its one nominal to yield:

(1*) John turned on the light by ([his] flipping the switch)

The sentence can now be regarded as split into function and argument, or put another way, as consisting of the subject term "[John's/his] flipping the switch" and the one-place predicate "John turned on the light by _____". Next, we regiment premise (3) to yield:

(3*) It is not the case that John turned on the light by ([his] turning on the light).

From these two "new" premises, (1*) and (3*), Goldman's desired conclusion,

(4) John's flipping the switch ≠ John's turning on the light,

rather straightforwardly drops out. I take it to be obvious from the preceding that nothing of value has been lost in this reconstruction of Goldman's argument. This reconstruction, then, serves to dispel the more immediate concerns one might have about structural requirements for the validity of Goldman's argument, given his own unfortunate remarks about the reasoning behind it.

Now I will proceed with my own criticisms of Goldman's argument. Let us turn to consider what support the premises might have. The remarks Goldman makes vis-à-vis the premises in his original argument are telling. With respect to premise (1)—that John turned on the light by flipping the switch—Goldman states, "We can *explain how* John turned on the light by indicating that he flipped the switch.... But we cannot explain how John flipped the switch by saying that he turned on the light...."[20] The latter sentence is also Goldman's support for premise (2), which I dispensed with in my reconstruction. Similarly in support of premise (3) Goldman remarks, "We would not say that John turned on the light by turning

---

20. Goldman, *A Theory of Human Action*, 5.

on the light....We cannot explain how John flipped the switch by indicating that he flipped the switch ...."[21]

These remarks reveal—what is not surprising—that these "by"-locutions employed by Goldman in his argument against Davidson constitute explanation contexts. This fact is enough to render the argument suspect, despite the structure we have unearthed, since by most accounts explanation contexts are notoriously nonextensional. However, undermining an argument on such general grounds puts one in the position of having to indicate both why Goldman's claims have their intuitive appeal and how they nevertheless go wrong or mislead.

Since the point of the first premise of the reconstructed Goldmanian argument is to introduce the example, it is for present purposes uncontroversial, and we must focus on the remaining premise,

(3*) It is not the case that John turned on the light by turning on the light.[22]

Admittedly, to say that John turned on the light by turning on the light is unusual, to say the least. Nonetheless I think there is a way of understanding such a claim in virtue of which it can be taken as expressing a truth. I do not know of a convincing way to show

---

21. Goldman, *A Theory of Human Action*, 5. Nonetheless in Raymond Queneau's novel, *The Flight of Icarus*, trans. Barbara Wright (London: Calder & Boyers, 1973), 30, we find this piece of dialogue:

    LN: Be on your guard! Be on your guard!
    ICARUS: But how?
    LN: By being on your guard!

22. I have dropped the regimenting punctuation and interpolation, its point having been made.

this directly, but I believe a case against (3*) can be made indirectly by attacking one of Goldman's other assumptions. Returning for a moment to Goldman's original argument, we find that he believes, for the case under discussion, that

(1) John turned on the light by flipping the switch

and

(1a) John flipped the switch by turning on the light

are incompatible. As we saw, his premise (2)—which is just the negation of (1a)—rested on the assumption that (1) is true and on his intuition that the purported relation involved is asymmetric. These in turn were supported by his claim, "We can *explain how* John turned on the light by indicating that he flipped the switch .... But we cannot explain how John flipped the switch by saying that he turned on the light...".

I believe that these underlying claims about what we can and cannot explain presume too much. What also has to be taken into account is the purpose such explanations are to play. We have already seen that the interests of the explainers and explainees play an important part in determining what may appropriately be said by way of explanation vis-à-vis particular cases.[23] In the present case this fact can be employed in a similar fashion to undermine the claim that (1) and (1a) are incompatible.

We can imagine two different explanations with regard to the same goings-on. Let John be an undercover narcotics officer meet-

---

23. See my arm-raising/signalling example in section 3.2.

ing some opium traffickers in a dingy warehouse. He knows that his fellow agents have built a transmitting device into the electrical circuits of the warehouse, but it has to be activated by flipping the light switch to the "on" position. He wonders how he will be able to flip the switch unobtrusively. Suddenly one of the traffickers curses and, getting to his hands and knees, mutters that he's dropped a contact lens. One of his minions strikes a match to assist the search. John, seeing his opportunity, ejaculates, "I'll get the lights," and moves to turn on the light, thereby, as his written report later explains, achieving his end of flipping the switch. This fable spells out a context for which (1a) would be an appropriate claim.

To make the compatibility of (1a) with (1) explicit, if it isn't obvious enough already, we can simply expand the story. Make one of the principals a primitive bushman who, in the circumstances, is intuitively aware that John's going to the wall and passing his arm over the surface somehow made the light go on, but being unacquainted with modern conveniences, has to have it pointed out to him that it was the flipping of the switch whereby John turned on the light.

It would be tempting here to resort to a Goldmanian style of reasoning and immediately infer from

(1) John turned on the light by flipping the switch

and

(1a) John flipped the switch by turning on the light

the desired conclusion that

(1/1a) John turned on the light by turning on the light.

But the unfortunate lack of appropriate singular terms is again a hurdle in our path. It is also a hurdle that in the present case cannot be leaped by the kind of regimentation previously employed. We can, however, proceed to reason obliquely as follows. Allowing the previous slack, we do have the singular terms of art "[John's] turning on the light" and "[John's] flipping the switch", which have singular reference to acts in the context provided by the example, given that (1) and (1a) are true. We may suppose that the pragmatics of the context imposes some ordering or relationship between these acts—a by-relation or a generational relationship, if you will—and furthermore makes the fact that such a relationship obtains sufficient (though not of course necessary) for the truth of the sort of "by"-locutions we have in (1) and (1a).

More specifically then, it might be said that there is some relation R such that the fact that R(John's turning on the light, John's flipping the switch) obtains is a sufficient condition for the truth of (1), and also such that the fact that R(John's flipping the switch, John's turning on the light) obtains is a sufficient condition for the truth of (1a). But if R is transitive, as Goldman has it,[24] then from

(i) R(John's turning on the light, John's flipping the switch)

and

(ia) R(John's flipping the switch, John's turning on the light)

24. Goldman, *A Theory of Human Action,* 20-21.

we can infer

(i/ia) R(John's turning on the light, John's turning on the light).

Then, by analogy with the earlier association of (i) with (1) and of (ia) with (1a), the fact that R(John's turning on the light, John's turning on the light) obtains would be a sufficient condition for the truth of

(1/1a) John turned on the light by turning on the light

despite the apparent unusualness of such a situation.

Thus, if my reasoning is correct, (1/1a) is established—i.e. premise (3*) in the reconstruction of Goldman's argument is rendered false—not on the basis of whether it itself would be appropriate to say in the context under consideration, but as a consequence of an analysis which states sufficient conditions for the truth of things [viz. (1) and (1a)] that would be appropriately said in that context.

Perhaps some case could independently be made for the falsity of a statement to the effect that John turned on the light by turning on the light. Such a case might be made on the basis of the statement's form of words being inherently unsuited to the task of explaining how John turned on the light, such explanation being a task purportedly undertaken when the "by"-locution is employed.

I must admit, as far as I can see this would only establish the triviality of such a statement outside the context of analysis. Remarks previously made in the discussion of the causal objection still apply. Davidson can simply deny that he is engaging in that sort of explanation when the statement in question, and other "by"-locutions generally, occur in the context of his theory. What Goldman would be denying would not be what Davidson is asserting (and vice versa), even though the same words might be used to express what is denied or asserted. Davidson can allow that it is not qua turning on the light that John's turning on the light explains how John turned on the light, without thereby contradicting the statement that John turned on the light by turning on the light.

Since the argument against Goldman's premise directly depends on the assumption of transitivity for R for its success, we must consider the implications of the possibility that Goldman might be willing to give up transitivity. However, if Goldman were to block the argument by this move, there is a backup argument involving no mention of transitivity we can employ against him. Let us reconsider the argument:

(1) John turned on the light by flipping the switch.

(3*) It is not the case that John turned on the light by turning on the light.

Therefore,

(4) John's flipping the switch ≠ John's turning on the light.

This time, however, instead of attacking (3*), let us take it to be true for the sorts of reasons having to do with explanatory role that Goldman advances, and furthermore let us assume it to be true because the following associated sufficient condition obtains:

(iii*) ¬ R(John's turning on the light, John's turning on the light).

As before, let us also assume that (1) is true because the sufficient condition

(i) R(John's turning on the light, John's flipping the switch)

obtains.

It is obvious that (1) and (3*) jointly entail (4) only if the sufficient conditions for (1) and (3*), viz. (i) and (iii*) respectively, also jointly entail (4). But do (i) and (iii*) jointly entail (4)? Let us consider Norvin Richards's example of a relation similar to R which has the same claims to asymmetry and irreflexivity that Goldman takes R to have:

> Consider Gerald Ford, the male occupant of the White House, the President of the United States, and the most powerful American citizen. Although these are indisputably the same person, a certain 'asymmetric and irreflexive' relation can be discerned here as well: that of being X by virtue of being Y. Although he is the most powerful American by virtue of being president, he is not president by virtue of being the most powerful American: that sounds like succession by *coup d'état*. And although he resides in the White House by virtue of being president, he is not president by virtue of residing there: that would be stranger still.
>
> As to irreflexivity, as Goldman says, "it would be odd to say that the man operates the pump *by* operating the pump". The same oddity attends saying Ford is president by virtue of being president....
>
> ...no one is moved thereby to give up calling Gerald Ford the same person as the most powerful American, the president, etc....[25]

From this passage we can extract an inference pattern parallel to the inference from (i) and (iii*), whose validity is in question. Let

25. Richards, "*E Pluribus Unum*: A Defence of Davidson's Individuation of Action", 192.

"S _____ _____ " =df "Gerald Ford is _____ by virtue of being _____". Then the parallel argument goes as follows:

(a) S (the most powerful American, the President).

(b) $\neg S$ (the President, the President).

Therefore,

(c) the President $\neq$ the most powerful American.

Since the falsity of the conclusion is compatible with the premises' being interpreted as true, this argument is invalid. Since we have no reason to believe that the nature of the relation involved in, and the structure of, the argument having (i) and (iii*) as premises and (4) as conclusion are in any relevant way different from that of this argument, we can only conclude that that argument is invalid as well. But if that argument is invalid, then the argument having (1) and (3*) as premises and (4) as conclusion must also be invalid, given that (i) and (iii*) are sufficient conditions for (1) and (3*) respectively.[26]

Let me recapitulate the conclusions of this examination of the relational objection. Despite claims to the contrary, it was shown that a certain logical structure required for validity can be discerned in Goldman's argument. Two arguments were then advanced to show that this was insufficient to establish the conclusion. First, by employing one of Goldman's own assumptions we showed one of his premises to be false and his argument unsound. Then a more general argument not relying on that assumption was adduced to show that Goldman's argument was not valid despite its apparent

---

26. This incidentally also shows that meeting Thomson's demand for paraphrase would not have been enough to validate Goldman's argument.

form. In passing, we also indicated how some of the Davidsonian claims could be understood as not antithetical to the intuitions underlying Goldman's claims.

Thus we may conclude that the argument from the by-relation poses no serious threat to Davidson, and can proceed to examine the temporal objection.

5.4 The Temporal Objection

Lastly, we come to subject the temporal objection to a closer scrutiny. The argument sustaining that objection, we will recall, may be represented as follows:

(1) Donald's shooting of Alvin took place 12 hours before Alvin's death.

(2) It is not the case that Donald's killing of Alvin took place 12 hours before Alvin's death.

Therefore,

(3) Donald's shooting of Alvin ≠ Donald's killing of Alvin.

What sorts of reasons are adduced in support of premise (2), the crucial premise in this argument? Goldman himself does not say much, but he does cite Lawrence H. Davis and Thomson. Turning to Davis, we find these remarks vis-à-vis a similar example:

> If the bullet wounded the prisoner, and the wound was obviously fatal, someone might have turned to me then and there and said "You killed him!"—even though he had not yet died. The propriety of such an exclamation suggests that my act of killing the prisoner was indeed already performed, though he was still alive....
>
> But the propriety of the exclamation supports Davidson's view in this way only if it is interpreted literally. And "You killed him!" interpreted literally appears to me to entail "He is dead." Since in the envisaged case he is not yet dead, I do not think we can take such an exclamation literally. I have in strict fact not yet killed him; though if and when he dies, I will have killed him.[27]

27. Lawrence H. Davis, "Individuation of Actions", *Journal of Philosophy* 67 (1970), 525. Also see Thomson, "The Time of a Killing", 120, where the same claim is expressed.

In the same work, Davis also claims:

> *If an act description entails that I brought some event about, the act it describes includes that event, any act by which I brought the event about, and any events causally linking such acts with that event.*[28]

Hints of this or a similar principle are also apparent in these remarks from Thomson:

> There are any number of true answers to the question when A killed B.
>   What I think we must say, however, is that there is no true answer to the question when A killed B that gives a time-stretch smaller than the minimal one that includes both the time of A's shooting of B and the time of the death of B....[29]
>
> ...the very thing that makes the time of completion of the killing be later than the time of completion of the shooting...is the fact that B dies after he is shot.[30]

The support for premise (2) in the temporal argument that can be extracted from these passages boils down to two claims. First, we have a claim that the notion of killing, as expressed by "kill" and its cognates, is so related to the notion of death, as expressed by "die" and its cognates, that literal statements of the form "X killed Y" entail statements of the form "Y is dead". This claim also has the corollary that examples of discourse which appear to suggest the contrary, i.e. that both "X killed Y" and "Y is not dead" are true, involve nonliteral uses of such expressions. Secondly, we have a claim that killings include the death in virtue of which they are

---

28. Davis, "Individuation of Action", 529.

29. Thomson, "The Time of a Killing", 122.

30. Thomson, "The Time of a Killing", 131-132.

killings. More briefly, we have (i) an entailment claim, with a corollary of nonliteralness to handle seeming counterexamples, and (ii) an inclusion claim.

Davis's principle above presumes an intimate connection between entailment and inclusion. But it is less than obvious, despite the intimations of their proponents, how these claims are related to one another.[31] Initially, then, I shall take up the inclusion claim, temporarily reserving judgment on the entailment claim.

The assumption that killings must include deaths has one quite curious result which is not expressly a result concerned with time as such. The last of Thomson's remarks above insinuates the idea that not only no shooting, but no action instrumental to a death at all can be a killing of the individual whose death it is. This indeed is what would follow from the claim that killings must include the deaths in virtue of which they are killings. If this consequence were so, I am not sure how we would handle certain kinds of cases which call for a distinction between death by natural causes and death by foul play. Imagine, for example, members of a forensic team conducting the following conversation over a corpse.

A: Do you think that he died of natural causes?

B: Not a chance. See that bruise behind his ear? What caused this death was definitely homicide.

This type of dialogue is common fare for those of us who are murder mystery fans, and is, I daresay, ordinary enough for philo-

31. In other domains of discourse, the claim that entities must include the entities presupposed by their descriptions would not even be taken seriously. A married man, for example, does not include his wife, despite the fact that she may be his "better half".

sophical purposes. And what is a homicide in such a context if not the killing of one human being by another?

Since causes don't cause themselves either in whole or in part, causes are distinct from their effects.[32] So an act or event which causes a death cannot include the death which is its effect. But the example just given provides a context for which it makes sense to allow that the cause of a death can be a homicide or a killing. So killings as such need not include deaths.[33] Thomson and Goldman do argue something to the effect that "kill" is not analyzable as, or does not mean the same as, "cause to die".[34] However, that response would not suffice here. All that it would establish is the possibility of deaths caused by things which are not killings, and not that no killing can be a cause of death.

Although it has, thus, been established that killings *need not* include the deaths in virtue of which they are killings, I think we can go for a stronger claim, viz. that for one paradigm of death, killings, as here understood,[35] *cannot* include the deaths in virtue of which they are killings.

In such indicative mood contexts as "X killed Y", the inflected verb form ending in "-ed" signals that the verb is in the nonprogressive past tense. Hence, if "X killed Y" describes an event or action, that event or action is one that was completed in the past, before the time of the description. The time of the description, we are

32. Parts of causes can of course cause *other* parts.

33. The alternative would be the absurdity of putting up with a second death to save the inclusion claim.

34. Thomson, "The Time of a Killing", 122; Goldman, "The Individuation of Action", 766, 768.

35. I make this caveat in order to exempt certain extended uses of "killing" discussed at the end of this section.

assuming, is also a time at which "*Y* is dead" is true. If so, it is conceivable that "*Y* is dead" might have been true for some while prior to that time, since "*Y* is dead (now) and has been for some time" is obviously not incoherent. On the other hand, if "*X* kills *Y*" correctly and truly described at some time prior to the present what is presently described by "*X* killed *Y*", then "*Y* is dead" could not have been true then, when "*X* kills *Y*" was true. That is to say, "*X* kills *Y*" is true only if "*Y* is not dead" is true[36]—a man already dead cannot be killed!

What follows from this is that the occurrence described by "*X* killed *Y*" takes place wholly before any moment at which "*Y* is dead" is true. However, before we can make any of these results relevant to the original objection from Goldman, we must determine how *Y*'s death fits into this scheme. The noun "death" as it appears in such expressions as "the death of *Y*", "*Y*'s death", "the moment of death", and so forth, I would suggest has no univocal sense, but is often vague and ambiguous. Consider the following sentences:

(1) Although his death was a long and painful one, when the moment of death came, there was a peaceful expression on his face.

(2) He had been dying of cancer for a long time, so the news of his death by suicide came as no surprise to me.

---

36. This is compatible with "*X* kills *Y*" entailing "*Y* will be dead", which I think does hold and is precisely where the progressive and nonprogressive tenses differ. Although "*X* kills *Y*" entails "*X* is killing *Y*" and each entails "*Y* is not dead", "*X* is killing *Y*" does not entail "*Y* will be dead", since someone can be engaged in killing and be stopped. I defend this in opposition to Jonathan Bennett's views later.

(3) The news of his dying early this morning took me by surprise, although others had known he was dying for quite some time.

(4) During the time a person dies, he often requires the comfort of family and friends.

(5) He is dying now and won't last much longer; there is no need for you to be here when he dies.

(6) In death, as in life, he was a financial burden to his family; the upkeep of his mausoleum was enormous.

(7) He was clinically dead on arrival, but soon after began to show vital signs again. Unlike many others in cases of this nature, he has made no claims about having had religious experiences during the period of his death.

An extensive analysis of the various notions of death and dying operative in these pieces of discourse cannot be undertaken here, but a few obvious points can be briefly made. (1) employs "death" both to indicate a longer process of dying ("his death") and perhaps something shorter like some last interval of this process ("the [extended] moment of death") when the cessation of life (= death?) was imminent, or perhaps the unextended moment at or after which the state of being dead occurs. (2) in addition to extended/unextended moment ambiguity for "his death", indicates the need to distinguish between being killed as one is dying and dying as one is being killed or as a result of one's being killed. (3) suggests process, extended moment, and unextended moment ambiguity for "dying" as well. (4) and (5) indicate similar ambiguity for "dies". (6) and (7) suggest a notion of death as a nonmomentary state of being dead which is going on when it is true to say of one that one is dead and which may even conceivably come to an end. There may be other notions of death as well, but the foregoing is sufficient to illustrate the problems involved in keeping discussion about death univocal.[37]

The notion of death indicated by (6) and (7) furnishes us with a reading of the claim that Donald's killing of Alvin occurred before Alvin's death, for which the stronger claim that killings cannot include deaths will hold. It has already been established that X could not have killed Y while it was the case that Y was dead. But if we take "Y's death" in the sense of (6) and (7) above, Y's death is just the ongoing state of Y's being dead, which occurs just in case it is true that Y is dead. In this sense, it is also the case that X could not have killed Y while his death was going on, and so Y's death must be wholly preceded[38] by the occurrence described by "X killed Y".[39]

This result, it will be noted, is still consistent with the entailment claim, since the killing may simply precede the death without there being any intervening moments of time for which "X killed

37. One notion we might also note is that "Y dies" or "Y's death occurs" may in gist say—to put it tenselessly—that at some moment Y is still alive and thereafter he is not, or at some moment Y is dead but therebefore he is not. Here there would be no moment of death per se but only one event followed by another. But in this sense the question of a death *included* in a killing could not even arise!

38. The notion of one event wholly preceding another deserves more comment than the pace of discussion here allows. I return to it in section 5.5.

39. Y can be dying, of course, while X kills him, but in my sense, Y's dying won't include Y's death either, since a dead man is not a dying man, nor a dying man a dead one.

Y" is true but "*Y* is dead" is not. However, the entailment claim, if correct, would still rule out a claim that Donald's killing of Alvin preceded Alvin's death by some moment or interval of time. We thus see that the inclusion claim was not so much interesting-but-false, as false-and-irrelevant for the purposes of the position advanced.

Since *pace* Davis the inclusion and entailment claims are independent after all, we must undermine the latter as well in order to support Davidson's position.

There is a kind of case which I think does afford a counterexample to the entailment claim. Imagine a Mafia boss turned informer for the district attorney. His life being in constant danger, he has an around-the-clock contingent of bodyguards to protect him in his penthouse suite and as he comes and goes between court sessions. The only time he is left unattended, for reasons of claustrophobia, is during the thirty second ride in the express elevator from the ground floor to his suite. During his last ride, the elevator ceiling opens, revealing a former underling who smiles and fires a bullet into our Mafia boss.

We might now imagine our Mafia boss saying a number of different things:

[*To the man who just shot him, apparently fatally*]

(8) So you have managed to kill me after all.

[*or*]

(9) So you have succeeded in killing me after all.

[*or*]

(10) So they have succeeded in having me killed after all.

[To his guards, as he falls through the elevator door]
(11) I didn't think I could be killed during those lousy thirty
seconds. *Merda...* I was wrong....
[Mumbles on a bit, then twitches and is motionless]

We can imagine to boot a certain kind of verbal exchange taking
place over these events—

The infuriated D.A. to the police lieutenant:

(12) How could you blow this? I thought your men were
watching him every second. When did they kill him?

The lieutenant replying:

(13) He was killed during the elevator ride, just after you
dropped him off. We tried to get the killer's identity
from him before he died, but he could only mumble.

These examples of speech considered in the context provided by
the accompanying story seem to suggest the possibility of there being times at which both an instance of "X killed Y" and "Y is not
dead", taken literally, are true; or at least suggest such possibility is
not obviously precluded.

(8)-(10) might be a bit contentious as far as this claim is concerned, but the possibility of their being true or coherent is surely
not in question. If true, however, they cannot entail that Y is dead,
for they are said by Y. What they do entail, I believe, is that Y will
be dead, since Y's not subsequently dying of the shot would be

sufficient to falsify the claims expressed by (8)-(10). What is at stake here is whether (8)-(10) are to be taken as literal or not, i.e. whether they entail, literally, "*X* (has) killed *Y*". They seem quite matter-of-fact to me, albeit dramatic, but then my intuitions may have been blunted by the pernicious influence of Hollywood and the Mystery Writers' Guild of America.[40] On the other hand, they do not seem to be straightforwardly figurative either.

Suppose the killer were to reply to any one of (8)-(10) with the quip, "Not yet"? Would we regard that as literal, or as a witty and ironical play on words? If the answer is the former, would we be willing to say the same of parallel cases? Consider the jailer who brought the prisoner his last meal. Could we say here that he didn't finish doing that until the prisoner was rendered incapable of ever eating again? And would we want to allow that the prisoner's response of "Not yet" to "Have you been brought your last meal already?" is incorrigibly true? Likewise, consider Sam who was the first of seventy-three invited guests to arrive. If he did not do this before the arrival of the seventy-third guest, in what literal sense was he first?

Perhaps though, it is best conceded that (8)-(10) are borderline cases. As such, I venture that the question of their status is properly raised not in relative isolation, but vis-à-vis a broader range of cases in the context of a semantic theory. Note, however, that even if such a theory rendered (8)-(10) nonliteral, that would only show that they could not be asserted literally in the pragmatic situation envisaged. Whether they might have true literal counterparts in the language of the theory is a different question from how the theory categorizes them as data.

---

40. Cf. Thomson, "The Time of a Killing", 120.

A stronger case for my contention is provided by (12) and (13). The indications here are that, while the Mafia boss Y is mumbling, both "X killed Y" and "Y is not dead" have to be true—even if at that time no one would quite say them together literally. To deny this would be tantamount to saying that (13) involved an inconsistency or was not an appropriate answer to the D.A.'s question. (13) is just an ordinary brass tacks response of the sort that a beleaguered police lieutenant might be expected to make in the circumstances. It even lacks the somewhat dramatic quality that might motivate a charge of nonliteralness in the case of (8)-(10).

We might add to the example and suppose that the D.A. himself had permitted the unattended elevator rides in an effort to keep the witness appeased and cooperative. Then he could understand the lieutenant's retort, "He was killed during the elevator ride", as also providing an excuse for himself (viz. he was not killed when *my* men were guarding him) and as shifting the blame (viz. he was killed during the lapse in security authorized by *you*). There is nothing nonliteral about these either said or merely understood statements containing "killed" as far as I can determine. Any killing that was done seems to have occurred in the elevator during the trip to the penthouse, whereas the death did not occur until several moments later in the suite.

Suppose further that the lieutenant actually had expressed the intimated subtextual sentiments out loud and the D.A. had responded, "What do you mean he wasn't killed while your men were in attendance and supposedly in control? Didn't he die right before their eyes?"—now *that* use of "killed", if it makes any sense at all with respect to my example, would indeed be nonliteral!

Indeed, the very supposition that the killer who killed the Mafia boss did not kill him in the elevator, during the thirty second ride to the penthouse, while the guards were not in attendance, has some odd consequences which would be a heavy price to pay for saving the entailment claim. Is the man who killed the Mafia boss still killing the Mafia boss after he shoots him? Certainly, since the shot turned out to be fatal, nothing remained to be done after that; and between the time he has fired the shot and the time Y dies, it seems false to say that he is killing Y. Fleeing the scene of the crime is surely not killing in this context. For X to be killing Y from a mile away requires technological resources beyond the handgun. The absurdity can be heightened by augmenting the example as follows: upon firing the fatal shot, the recoil causes X to plunge down the elevator shaft to his own death, such that he ends up dead minutes before the Mafia boss. If he were still killing the latter in any literal sense after that, it would be a case for exorcism.

In the wake of the foregoing, I think it in order to pass over (11), which has not been discussed so far, with a quick, perhaps merely suggestive remark. My suggestion, for the context envisaged, is that since the Mafia boss is not a philosopher, the basis for his apparently true claim that his previous belief was wrong is best cast not as an on-the-spot piece of *a priori* reasoning, but as an *ab esse ad posse* inference.

What the foregoing discussion of the shooting-killing example establishes, minimally, is that there is one event which is a shooting at t and can be truly asserted to be a killing at t' later than t. In short, the strongest support for my claim that the shooting *is* the killing seems to come from considerations of what can truly (or more smoothly) be said with hindsight later. So, one might ask, why not go the extra step and make not only the assertibility conditions but also the truth conditions of what is asserted a function of time?

Jonathan Bennett seems to have adopted such a tactic. His verdict on the shooting-killing example is that there is one event which is a shooting at t and which *becomes* a killing at t' later than t.[41] Both answers thus allow the event which is a killing somehow to be identified with the event which is a shooting and to that extent there is nothing to choose between. However Bennett's solution entails that 'if as A is shooting B someone says "A is killing B," and in fact B does not die until several hours later, then what the speaker says is false'.[42] I am not committed to this, nor do I find it persuasive. In fact I do not even believe that B needs to die at all for "A is killing B" to be true.

Before I present my case for this, let me avert possible confusion by emphasizing what is at issue here. We are concerned with the use of the present progressive tense ("is killing"), and not with various uses of the simple past or the past and present perfect tenses ("killed", "have managed to kill", etc.). Because the latter uses involve verbs ending in "-ed", they carry the suggestion of completed action (as the grammar books say), whereas the use of progressive forms does not. This being so, the unease that previously led us to postpone a decision on the status of (8)-(10) need not carry over to support Bennett's particular contention here.

Let us imagine a situation where a couple of police officers walking their beat are beckoned from a doorway by a distraught child: "Come quick! Please! My pop's killing my mom!" Immediately entering the premises, they find the father choking the mother, and hear her rasp, "Stop...you're killing me...." The officers disengage the pair and the mother is saved. Later in the precinct station the officers recount the events of their shift: "When we burst in this guy was killing his wife...."

---

41. Jonathan Bennett, "Shooting, Killing and Dying", *Canadian Journal of Philosophy* 2 (1973), 316.

42. Bennett, "Shooting, Killing and Dying", 320.

I do not see why any of these pieces of discourse *must* be false. The presumed truth of the child's present tense report seems to be the only reason for the officer's swift action, since they have no other information to go on. As for the mother's plea, we might by way of contrast think of the same words uttered under different circumstances; for instance, during a vicious but merely verbal domestic dispute, or even during the telling of an egregious shaggy-dog story. A natural way of distinguishing the mother's use from these uses would be to say that she means "*literally* killing"; it is difficult to see this as naive. If the child and mother spoke truly, the officer's past tense statement follows suit so far as it recapitulates the same claim about the father's action.

Now it might be objected that although true, these statements are elliptical, i.e. that strictly speaking the father was not killing his wife, but merely *trying* or *attempting* to kill her. Need this be granted? I think not. For the mother even in her direst straits could believe—surely coherently, hence possibly truly—that her husband doesn't really mean to do what he is doing (alas, such is often the nature of domestic disputes). In fact in the absence of somesuch belief her plea could not easily be construed as advancing a reason for him to stop.

But this objection is actually a red herring, since no one believes that there cannot be unintentional killing. An easier way of meeting it would be simply to stipulate that the father is a zombie. The real issue concerns not trying but failing.

Can there be killing without success? Here we might note a parallel in the act of cleaning. One can be cleaning an object, and while doing this be interrupted and attracted to something else. If one doesn't return to finish the job, then the object won't be clean. Although one hasn't cleaned the object, one will have been cleaning it nevertheless. "*A* is cleaning *B*" can be true even if *B* is never clean. Moreover there is a difference between cleaning an object and trying to clean it, this difference being largely a matter of how well one's cleaning is going, unless of course it's a matter of getting started at all.

All that seems to be required for cleaning to occur is that the action involved have (or be of the sort that typically has) the *propensity* to result in a clean object. I contend that, mutatis mutandis, such is the case with killing as well.

When circumstances do not permit such actions to be performed with brevity, we should think of cleaning and killing as tantamout to processes. In our mom-and-pop example, for instance, the police officers could equally well have said, "When we burst in this guy was *in the process* of killing his wife...." While the verbs labelling such actions do suggest outcomes, they don't guarantee them for particular actions. Processes can end prematurely—while in process, as we say. The father in our example is in the process of killing his wife, but the police manage to cut the process short.

To be sure, cleaning and killing do differ in at least one important respect. It is seldom obvious that someone is in the process of killing in the way that it is obvious that someone is in the process of cleaning. (This is a matter of degree, though.) Hence a claim of the form "*A* is killing *B*" is more likely to be unwarranted and eo ipso rightly regarded with suspicion.

There are many ways the claim "*A* is killing *B*" might be mistaken. The action of the person who seeks to kill just may not be of a sort having real potential to produce death; but we may not be able to tell this just by looking. A choke-hold needs to be applied with a certain minimum of pressure to have this potential, but this will vary from victim to victim. Yet even when done viciously and with enough pressure, choking may not be killing if under the particular circumstances it's very unlikely to produce death[43]—good torturers unlike irate husbands may know exactly how far they can go. In any such case, knowledge of whether appropriate causal relationships and potentials do obtain is just plain hard to come by. So it goes without saying that an immediately ensuing death in hand would be the best possible evidence we could have that "*A* is killing *B*" was true. But ease of verification scores no conceptual points.

Before bringing this discussion of the temporal objection to a close, there is one last item that requires comment. I have so far shown that the inclusion assumption for what constitutes a killing is necessarily false for one central notion of death and perhaps contingently false for other notions as well. Likewise it has been demonstrated that the entailment claim is false, independent of what notion of death (from the various possibilities suggested) is involved. Nothing, however, has been said about various notions of killing that might be expressed by "kill" and its cognates; I have more or less taken univocality for granted. It would be foolhardy, however, for me to make the strong claim that no notion at all of killing as including death can be discerned in or extracted from the way we speak. When an event is designated in a newspaper as a killing and *its* details are reported, these details may include details of the death. Here the description of the killing could also subsume a description of the death, so there is some sense in which it could be said of such a case that the killing includes the death.[44] It wouldn't

---

43. It may be that even when an action does produce death, it may be too extreme to consider it a killing if the causal sequence is very attenuated. Recall the discussion in section 5.2 over whether "kill" means "cause the death of".

44. Such subsumption is of course as common as dirt. Consider for example the expression "Sadat's trip to Israel", which to most people obviously refers to more than would be described by Sadat's response to "How was your trip here, Mr. Sadat?" upon disembarking at the Tel Aviv airport.

do for a normally overzealous reporter to excuse his failure to write up the death on the grounds that his editor had told him, "This time, write up *just* the killing."[45]

I suspect that many cases of this nature would best be viewed as involving extended uses of "death" and "killing", since they are quite amenable to analysis in terms of such standard tropical categories as metonymy and synecdoche. However, even if theoretical considerations require such uses to be construed as entirely literal I do not think my arguments will be affected. Whether or not a case can be made for some use of the nominalization "the killing" where the death involved is included in the referent, if there were such a case of killing, it would not and could not be the sort of thing described—namely an action—by instances of "X kills Y", "X killed Y", "X was killing Y", and the like. And these are after all the killings we are concerned with.

This concludes my reconsideration of the temporal objection to Davidson's identity thesis. To sum up, my treatment of the temporal objection to the identity thesis has accomplished three things. First, it has shown that the entailment and inclusion claims are independent. Secondly, it has, like Bennett's treatment, shown that the temporal objection, insofar as its success depends on such claims, can be met by a unifying approach to event individuation. Thirdly, it has, unlike Bennett's solution, avoided a certain prima facie undesirable commitment.

Having thus disposed of all three standard objections to Davidson's position, we are at last free to turn to other matters. In

---

45. Equally, though, a headline might proclaim the occurrence of a death, with the description that follows consisting mostly of gory details of the process of killing which led to the death. Would there then be a death which includes a killing?

the next chapter we will address the suspicion that the unifier-multiplier dispute might in some sense not be over substantive issues.

5.5 Postscript

In the discussion above I expressed one of my conclusions by employing the notion of "one event wholly preceding another". Although this notion is not really problematic, its subtleties may not be immediately apparent. So I think it would be illuminating to indicate the ways in which one event might wholly precede another and how these ways tie in with the entailment and inclusion claims.

I will take it for granted that "*d* precedes *e* in time" is clear enough preanalytically: roughly, *d* is in progress before *e* is. The purpose of the adverb "wholly" in "*d* wholly precedes *e*" is to ensure that there is no moment of time at which both *d* and *e* are occurring. (*In situ*, that meant that there is no moment at which *Y* was both being killed by *X* and dead.) I will also assume the standard practice of using the real number line to represent time; moments of time will then be analogous to points on the line, and periods of time, to intervals. Accordingly, we can now show that the relationship involved in one occurrence wholly preceding another admits of seven cases vis-à-vis the interface between *d* and *e:*

Case (i) ⋯

> where *t* is the last moment of event *d,* and *t'* is the first moment of event *e*. Here there will of necessity be a temporal gap between *d* and *e* because there is an infinite number of points between any two points on the real number line.

Case (ii) ⋯

where *t* is the last moment of *d*, but *e* has no first moment;
however, for any arbitrary point *t′* at which *e* is occurring, *e* will be occurring at every moment between *t′* and
t.

Case (iii)

The diagram is the same as for case (ii), except that *t′* is the
first moment of *e*, and *d* has no last moment; however,
for any arbitrary point *t* at which *d* is occurring, *d* will
be occurring at every moment between *t* and *t′*.

Case (iv) ⋯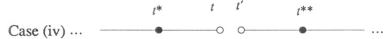

where *d* does not have a last moment, and *e* does not have a
first moment. However there is a point *t* at which *d* is
not occurring such that for any arbitrary point *t** at
which *d* is occurring, *d* is occurring at all points
between *t** and *t*; likewise, there is a point *t′* at which *e*
is not occurring such that for any arbitrary point *t*** at
which *e* is occurring, *e* is occurring at all points between
t′ and *t***.

Case (v) ⋯   ──────────────○────────────── ⋯

is like case (iv), except that *t* and *t′* are one and the same
point. Here there is no temporal delay, as such, between
d and *e*; but they are "separated" by an instant or moment of time (a "point gap").

Case (vi) ··· ─────────────────○ ●───────────────── ···

Case (vii) ··· ─────────────────● ○───────────────── ···

> in light of the preceding cases, I assume these two diagrams are self-explanatory, and note only that there is in each case a gap between d and e.

The entailment claim, if correct, would rule out all cases but (ii) and (iii) for d = the event described by "X killed Y" and e = Y's death. In all cases exclusive of (ii) and (iii) there exist between d and e moments or intervals of time for which "X killed Y" is true but "Y is dead" is not. Since these five cases cover all the ways an event might conceivably precede another by some time gap—with case (v) thrown in as a limit case—the entailment claim does directly rule out the Davidsonian claim that Donald's killing of Alvin preceded Alvin's death by 12 hours. The inclusion claim, if correct, would rule out not only the cases ruled out by the entailment claim, but (ii) and (iii) as well. This is so because the inclusion claim requires that for d = the killing and e = the death, d and e have points in common—more specifically, that all the points of e are points of d—and such a state of affairs is not covered by our diagrams.[46]

Since the inclusion and entailment claims make different pronouncements with respect to our diagrams, we have in them a graphic illustration of the independence of these two claims.

46. So there is no

Case (viii) ··· ─────────────●───────────── ···

which is like case (i), except that $t=t'$. Since here d and e overlap or merge at t, the word "wholly" would not apply.

6

IS THE DISPUTE REAL?

6.1 Comparative Phraseology

One of the strategies we used in defusing Goldman's arguments against Davidsonian identity claims involved providing alternative ways of understanding claims denied by key premises in these arguments. That such moves are possible indicates that there is an element of the merely verbal involved in the unifier-multiplier dispute; for part and parcel of such a move is the presumption that what the one disputant takes certain key statements to assert need not be what is denied by the other.[1] Considerations such as this one, and others I will go into below, force one to raise the question of whether or not the unifier-multiplier dispute is a dispute over substantive mat-

---

1. There are of course real disputes which, because they are about words, are in a sense "verbal" as well. Some disagreements about the facts of linguistic usage fall into this category. Verbal disputes of this sort are not my concern here. What I wish to be conveyed by my use of the phrase "merely verbal" is in part a notion of failure in understanding what is at issue.

ters;[2] i.e. whether the alleged differences over central issues are "real" or whether upon closer inspection they will reveal themselves as merely verbal or perhaps trivial in some other way.

Now such nonsubstantive differences as we have previously encountered between unifiers and multipliers are suggestive but do not of themselves establish that the unifier-multiplier dispute as such is not genuine. Although mere verbal disagreement about particular examples might be linked to mere verbal disagreement at a more fundamental level, it might also *not* be so linked: one can after all imagine two unifiers or two multipliers having conflicting intuitions about a particular case too. The important thing is what theoretical views are drawn from or held in common with such intuitions. In order to show that the unifier-multiplier dispute itself is not a substantive dispute one would have to show that the main theses associated with the unifying and multiplying approaches are not really opposed to each other except in trivial ways.

We can begin by taking up two sorts of considerations that might be advanced as showing that unifiers and multipliers are not in genuine opposition. One might show that the accounts are really about different things, i.e. that they complement each other, with confusion perhaps arising from the fact that similar forms of words are employed to talk about quite different things. Alternatively, or additionally, one might show that although quite different forms of

---

2. Sentiments to the effect that the dispute is not a substantive one have been voiced sporadically in the philosophical literature, though generally not with much elaboration. Thalberg, for example, speaks of various approaches to events and actions as different "language games" in his "Singling Out Actions, Their Properties and Components", 787. Hector–Neri Castañeda, "Intensionality and Identity in Human Action and Philosophical Method", *Noûs* 13 (1979), section 1, views the identity of actions as a nonissue. Also see Kim's remarks quoted in the next section.

words are used, they are nevertheless used to draw the same distinctions and are in some sense intertranslatable.

Let us see, then, to what extent a comparison between various aspects of the two accounts is possible. As a point of departure, let us take up Goldman's remark that his 'fine-grained method of act-individuation cannot justly be accused of "increasing the furniture of the world"' because it does not countenance any entities not admitted by Davidson's account.[3]

One picture this suggests is that we have a store of acts or events in the presumed ontologies of both theories, some of which seem to be intimately related to one another—the "unity" spoken of in a previous chapter. Davidson says the relationship is one of identity. Goldman and (by alliance) Kim say it is generation.

Now there is an ambiguity in the preanalytical notions of "things done" and "things that happened" that allows us to identify such "things" either with some one thing which has many aspects (or is of many types), or with the many aspects of some one thing (or types it falls under). Such ambiguity could conceivably lie in back of what appear to be points of difference between unifiers and multipliers, as for example the one just cited in the preceding paragraph. Is it the case that this ambiguity *is* reflected in the two accounts?

What is the connection between an expression of the form "$d = e$" in Davidson's theory and of the form "d generates e" in Goldman's theory? To answer this question we need to know what sorts of things the respective "d"s and "e"s pick out. Let us assume

---

3. Goldman, *A Theory of Human Action*, 8-9. Strictly speaking, Goldman's claim here is just plain false. Not only has he got more acts and events in his ontology than a unifier needs to have, but more kinds of things: act-trees, various generation relations, an exemplification relation, properties, and times. I think that his claim must be charitably understood as a claim about event multiplication per se.

that the "d" in the first expression picks out the same thing as the "d" in the second expression, i.e. that the terms are univocal. Ditto for "e". If the dispute here is merely verbal, then there ought to be a reading which makes both "$d = e$" and "d generates e" true. Within the constraints just specified, that comes to a semantic interpretation which satisfies both "=" and "generates". Since the former is an equivalence relation and the latter avowedly is not, there can be no such reading, and hence no merely verbal difference at this interface.

It might however be claimed that this comparison is too simplistic. The comparison should not be between "$d = e$" and "d generates e", but between "$d = e$" and something like "d is generationally connected to e", where events related by chains of generation or its inverse are covered as well. Thus one who believes the two theories compatible might advance the position that $d = e$ in Davidson's scheme of things if and only if d is generationally connected to e in Goldman's scheme of things. Ceteris paribus, that would make for the extensional equivalence of the opposed explanatory relations. Those partial to set theoretic abstractions might be disposed on this ground to wonder what all the fuss was about.[4]

Such a reaction, I will suggest is too quick for two reasons. One is that generation-connectedness is simply too broad a notion. It relates events which would *not* be countenanced as identical by Davidson. Examples of this can be developed easily enough if one focuses on compound generation (the subspecies of augmentation generation). As things stand, there is nothing that bars events that Davidson would take to stand in a part-whole relationship rather

4. The author is reminded of a tiresome conversation in which Thomas Hurka glibly declaimed, "*Of course* the whole issue is trivial since both accounts partition events into the same equivalence classes."

than identity from being generationally connected in Goldman's scheme.[5]

But even ignoring this factor, it is difficult to see a correspondence between the theories in these terms for still another reason. The comparison as stated above leaves out an important fact, viz. that identity claims are after all made in Goldman's account as well as in Davidson's account, and that Goldman and Davidson unarguably agree on some identity claims. Consequently the broader notion of generational connection among events, if there is to be such a notion for the purposes of comparison, will have to encompass some cases of identity. Thus "d is generationally connected to e" will have to be unpacked as "(d generates e & $d \neq e$) or (d is generated by e & $d \neq e$) or $d = e$".[6] A consideration of extensional equivalence would have some force in deemphasizing putative differences between Davidson and Goldman if at least one of the two relations in question were a purely theoretical term. But as is now obvious with the introduction of identity into Goldman's explanatory relation, such is not the case. After all, both unifiers and multipliers, to adapt Prior's mot, are interested in "real identity" when they make their respective claims, and not some abstractional surrogate for identity.[7] "Identity" is univocal across both accounts.

Since—under the proposal we are examining—Davidson's identity is extensionally equivalent to generational connection, it is eo ipso not extensionally equivalent to Goldman's identity. Since Davidson's identity is neither extensionally the same as nor just a

5. See Donald Davidson, "Causal Relations", *Journal of Philosophy* 64 (1967), 698-699 <157>.

6. Actually both instances of the conjunct "$d \neq e$" are redundant, given what we know of the meaning of "generates".

7. A.N. Prior, *Objects of Thought* (Oxford: Clarendon Press, 1971), 64.

homonym of Goldman's identity, there is a genuine disagreement over what things are in fact identical.

Another ploy that might be tried in arguing for lack of genuine rivalry between Davidson and Goldman is to withhold the assumption of univocality for the corresponding "*d*"'s and "*e*"'s in the two initial expressions. That is to say, the "*d*" in "*d = e*" and the "*d*" in "*d* generates *e*" are to be understood as appropriate to different kinds of things, perhaps the event-*d* in the former case, and the property-exemplification-*d* in the latter (ditto for "*e*").[8] If this were so, then apparent rivalry could be explained in terms of the ambiguity of "*d*" (or "*e*"). However, the multiplying-generational theory makes a further claim, viz. that actions and events are just property-exemplifications by an agent or object at a time. If this were simply a stipulation, then the two accounts could be about different subject matters, and their differences merely verbal. However the claim as made, I take it, presumes to be more interesting than this, and insofar as it is, we again have a genuine rivalry at this interface between the two accounts.[9]

There is another suggestion we might consider. While expressing the previously noted view that both his and Davidson's schemes are attempts to account for the unity among diverse acts, Goldman himself makes the following comparison:

> Having developed techniques for individuating and interrelating acts of various kinds, we might pause to notice that our scheme provides a fairly natural way of interpreting the sort of thing which Anscombe and Davidson would regard as a "single" action.... Now Anscombe's or

8. Cf. Thalberg, "Singling Out Actions, Their Properties and Components", 787: "Goldman seems engaged in...cataloguing properties exemplified during some phase of an agent's career.... But perhaps Goldman imagines that individuating them amounts to individuating the deeds in which they are manifested."

9. Cf. Goldman, *A Theory of Human Action*, 10.

Davidson's notion of a single action, I think, corresponds to our notion of a single act-tree. Their single *action* corresponds to the set of all acts on a single *act-tree*, or perhaps to whatever "underlies" the acts on a single act-tree.... Their notion of a single action is an intuitively attractive one, however, and it is important to see that some such notion can be captured and expressed within our framework.[10]

In the light of such remarks, it could be thought that the proper unit of comparison for Davidson's events is not Goldman's property-exemplifications but rather the trees on which the generationally related property-exemplifications are generated.

It is certainly understandable why there might arise an initial temptation to equate actions or events with trees if they do indeed play similar roles, as Goldman seems to be suggesting. However, a consideration similar to that which precluded the dispute from being spurious in the last case also applies here: for Goldman, actions and events are property-exemplifications, not trees. This I believe settles the matter. Nonetheless, for someone interested in revising or synthesizing the accounts, an identification of events with trees would be a natural enough point of departure. So it may be of some value to note some additional points of difference between Goldman's trees and Davidson's events. Let me briefly mention a couple that may present difficulties.

We might start by noting the fact that events are things that happen, take place, or occur. There seems to be no way of saying the same for trees except derivatively, insofar as the entities represented by the nodes happen, take place, or occur. Perhaps Goldman's notion of 'whatever "underlies" the acts on a single act-tree' might be accounted for in a way that would allow us to speak of it in the same terms as actions and events. But then one wonders how this would

---

10. Goldman, *A Theory of Human Action* , 37.

square with Goldman's tenet that actions and events are exhausted by the property-exemplifications that are the elements of his trees.

The quoted passage also suggests that a common ground between events and trees might be specified in terms of sets. Goldman's trees are indeed very setlike entities—his idioms ("tree", "branching") seem to be more descriptive of the diagrammatic notation than of the ontological status of what is represented thereby. However, if trees do have the status of sets, as seems likely, it is clear that what Davidson regards as a single action is not a set or setlike entity.[11]

There is another way of developing this set theoretic angle. One could speak cavalierly of "Davidson's notion of a single act" as sets of acts which are the extensions of identity relations, and then attempt to identify these sets with trees or sets of acts which are the extensions of generation relations. But this angle is one we have already covered.

So it appears that an easy comparison between the two accounts, in the terms so far considered, is not in the offing. Here I think Goldman was wise not to claim more than loose correspondences between his and Davidson's accounts.

11. This is strikingly borne out by Davidson's evaluation of the property-exempli-fication criterion in his "The Individuation of Events", 223 <170>: "The effect is to substitute for what I think of as particular, dated events classes of such, and thus to make the identities harder to come by."

6.2 Some Facts About Values

Another suggestion of lack of genuine opposition between the theories underlying the unifying and multiplying approaches comes, surprisingly, from Kim himself:

> ...it seems to me that there are no irreconcilable *doctrinal* differences between Davidson's theory of event discourse as a semantical theory and the property exemplification account of events as a metaphysical theory.[12]

However, whether or not we are to understand this remark as a verdict on the unifier-multiplier dispute is a moot point. I will suggest that Kim's remark, occurring as it does in the context of a continuing dialogue on event individuation which can be traced back to Anscombe, might plausibly be taken in either of two ways. I will shortly indicate these. One I will comment on only briefly, for it will be dealt with in the next chapter. The other, I will go on to argue, is false.

But first a few words by way of explanation are required. The background of the quoted remark is this. Kim has just made the historical point that part of Davidson's motivation in theorizing about events as particulars can be traced to his concern for representing the logical form of action-describing sentences containing adverbial modifiers, or more specifically, his concern for representing certain entailments among such sentences.[13] This representation was accomplished by introducing variables for events into the regimented versions of such sentences.

---

12. Kim, "Events as Property Exemplifications", 167.

13. Davidson, "The Logical Form of Action Sentences", 81ff <105ff>.

One of the things that Kim has in mind above is that his and Goldman's property-exemplifications, represented by something of the form "[*agent/object, property, time*]", can serve as the *values* of Davidson's event variables. This does not seem like an implausible suggestion, and for the time being we won't question it.[14] However, this remark is immediately followed up with the additional claim:

> True enough, Davidson and I disagree about particular cases of individuation of events; for example, whether Brutus's stabbing Caesar is the same as Brutus's killing Caesar. But most of these differences about particular cases seem traceable to possible differences in our views about causation, explanation, and intensionality.[15]

Two points can be made. First, this second remark suggests an illegitimate transfer of the observation made in the first remark into a domain where it does not belong. The disagreement over particular cases occurs in contexts where Davidson is no longer concerned with representing entailments but with the identity and individuation of events per se. This latter concern and its ontological ramifications do not stand or fall with his views on logical form. Yet it is expressly in those contexts not dealing directly with logical-cum-se-

---

14. Some difficulties facing Kim in developing logical machinery to accommodate such structures are pointed out by R.M. Martin, "Events and Actions: Some Comments on Brand and Kim", in *Action Theory*, ed. M. Brand and D. Walton (Dordrecht-Holland: D. Reidel Publishing Co., 1976), 188-189.

15. F.E. Sparshott, *Looking for Philosophy* (Montreal and London: McGill Queens University Press, 1972), 21, 168, characterizes a certain species of riddle as "seeming conundrums with irregular answers". It is amusing to note that Kim's remarks might easily be cast as an answer to such a riddle. Cf. Sparshott's own example of this type of riddle:
Q: Why is Winston Churchill like Father Christmas?
A: They both have beards, except Winston Churchill.

mantic theory, as we saw in the treatment of the three main objections to Davidson's unifying approach, that the differences about causation, explanation, and intensionality come into play.

Secondly, the fact that the dispute between Davidson and the multipliers can be seen to turn on other issues is a long way from its being self-evidently the case that there is no real rivalry. To show *that* would require showing that those issues as well involve no "irreconcilable differences", and this is by no means obvious.

The second point brings us to the two ways of taking Kim's remark I mentioned earlier. Now although the dispute between unifiers and multipliers is primarily a dispute about the individuation of events as it relates to Anscombe's "how many?" question, it is clear that much more than that is at stake. In advancing the particular individuation claims, other theses are explicitly or implicitly relied upon. The Goldman-Kim multiplying position, for example, involves a number of interrelated positions with respect to existence conditions, identity criteria, and certain linguistic matters.

With such considerations in mind what we have to decide is whether Kim's statement is to be taken as a remark on the unifier-multiplier debate in all its complexity or not.

If not, we can take the import of Kim's claim as being an observation to the effect that Davidson has said nothing which specifically precludes events from being property-exemplifications, so for all we know Davidson's events might be property-exemplifications. I think this, as far as it goes, is a correct view of things and will return to it in the next chapter.

On the other hand, if we take the claim as having a broader import with respect to the unifier-multiplier debate, I think Kim is on shakier ground. The considerations about causality, explanation, etc. used to substantiate the various arguments against Davidson's identities and to advance the multipliers' ontological scheme do so by establishing a much stronger "semantic tie" between event descriptions of a certain kind[16] and their descripta than Davidson would allow.

As Kim himself phrases it, there are certain descriptions which might be taken as "canonical" in that they tell us what the constitutive object, property, and time of an event are, and knowing this "*is to know what that event is*."[17] This is not a stipulation but a substantive claim about the relationship of certain linguistic items to the world.

To take a paradigmatic example, as far as our particular multipliers are concerned a statement like "John turned on the light at noon" can only describe the property-exemplification [John, turning on the light, noon][18] and not some other property-exemplification such as [John, flipping the switch, noon]. Of course any disagreement over such claims concerning what properties are and are not involved in the descripta of certain event descriptions will in a sense be a dispute about words. But upon pain of trivializing the multipliers' account, it will not be a merely verbal dispute. Insofar as the disagreements over individuation are a reflection of disagreements over the semantic tie between descriptions and descripta—and it is

16. It is not clear what marks off this kind from others. But see Goldman, *A Theory of Human Action*, 11-12, and Kim, "Events as Property Exemplifications", 167-168; then cf. Thalberg, "Singling out Actions, Their Properties and Components", especially section 2.

17. Kim, "Events as Property Exemplifications", 166. However he acknowledges that an account of constitutive properties ("generic events") needs to be provided (169).

18. This claim, being metalinguistic, is not simply a restatement of the Goldman-Kim existence condition for events; but it might be regarded as embodying an intuition sustaining that condition.

hard to see how it could be otherwise—those disagreements will be real as well.[19]

This difference between the two accounts also has consequences for Kim's suggestion vis-à-vis Davidson's logical-cum-semantic theory. Given the Goldman-Kim line on the descripta of certain descriptions, the claim that their property-exemplifications can serve as the values of Davidson's event variables turns out to be rather specious.

I do not propose to go into a detailed exposition of Davidson's logical analysis of event sentences here. But an example will serve to illustrate of what limited value Kim's claim really is. Consider the following sequence of sentences said of some particular occasion:

(1) John did a despicable thing.

(2) He flipped the switch in the bedroom.

(3) He turned on the light while George and Mary were being indiscreet.

19. Here one might ask, can one decide the unifier-multiplier dispute without deciding first what events ontologically speaking are like, and if one can, would the dispute be purely verbal? My answer to the first question is divided. It is "yes", if the suggestion is that one must have a specific account of the nature of events in hand—my defence of Davidson attests to that answer. However, if the suggestion is that we need not assume anything whatsoever about events, it would have to be "no". Some minimal assumptions about the descripta of event locutions have to be made; for example, their typical involvement with objects and properties, their entering into causal relations, and so forth.

The second answer to the first question also answers the second question: the sense in which we can decide the individuation dispute without first deciding what events are, is not a sense in which the dispute is independent of things in the world.

A final remark. My use of the expression "descripta of event locutions" is deliberately cagey, for I wish to leave open the possibility that at some level the unifier-multiplier dispute need not even take the irreducibility of events for granted. This will be discussed in the next chapter.

Suppose further that there is some logical connection between these sentences and another sentence uttered on the same occasion,

(4) John did something despicable in the bedroom while George and Mary were being indiscreet.

How would Davidson represent all this? Here is a typical analysis, with existential quantification over event variables to reveal the logical connection:

(5) $(\exists x)$ [did(John, x) & despicable(x) & flipped(John, the switch, x) & in(the bedroom, x) & turned on (John, the light, x) & while George and Mary were being indiscreet(x)] $\rightarrow$ $(\exists y)$ [did(John, y) & in(the bedroom, y) & while George and Mary were being indiscreet (y)].

More or less structure can be shown of course, depending on what entailments or material relationships one wishes to make manifest. The germane point here is that one event variable in the antecedent and consequent each is sufficient to capture an intuitive interconnection between (1)-(3) and (4). However—if Goldman and Kim are consistent—there is no one property-exemplification that they can accept as a value for "x" throughout (let alone both "x" and "y"). On their view, for example, (2) would have to describe the property-exemplification [John, flipped the switch in the bedroom, while George and Mary were being indiscreet], whereas (3) would have to describe the property-exemplification [John, turned on the light, while George and Mary were being indiscreet]. Thus the suggestion that such structures can serve as the values of Davidson's event variables carries with it the consequence that much of the logical structure that Davidson would want to display would be either precluded or only representable via variables for which no property-exemplification à la Goldman and Kim—and hence no event?—could count as a value. This, *pace* Kim, seems to me to involve a "doctrinal difference" of a fundamental sort.

In this chapter we have entertained various considerations and arguments that might be advanced to show that the unifier-multiplier dispute is spurious. At key interfaces where the suggestion of lack of genuine rivalry appeared strongest we nevertheless uncovered substantive differences between the two accounts. I do not believe that the differences we found are the only substantive differences; but they are sufficient to lay to rest the view that there is no genuine rivalry between unifiers and multipliers over fundamental matters.

7

FINAL WORDS ON THE MULTIPLIERS

7.1 Summary

We began with a consideration of two contending approaches to the individuation of actions and other events, viz. the unifying approach and the multiplying approach. The unifying approach, identified with Davidson, allows one and the same event to be described variously by means of expressions that may ascribe or attribute different event properties to it. The multiplying approach, identified with Goldman and Kim, maintains that event-describing expressions that ascribe or attribute different event properties ipso facto describe different events. In short (and in rough), the unifying approach allows one event under many descriptions while the multiplying approach allows only one description over an event.

Three major objections were raised against the unifying approach: a causal objection, a relational objection, and a temporal objection. These seemed prima facie quite devastating to the unifying approach in its specific applications, and were offered as the major motivation for adopting a multiplying approach as alternative.

Davidson's approach had provided an explanation of the unity of events under various descriptions in terms of identity. Goldman's multiplying account sought to do the same in terms of a technical notion of generation, while avoiding the purported objectionable consequences of Davidson's approach. On closer examination it was discovered that Goldman's account was itself not able to avoid the difficulties raised by the three objections and faced additional problems besides. Furthermore, it was subsequently shown that Goldman's account was not amenable to modifications that would enable it to sidestep these difficulties.

Next, the three objections against Davidson were reconsidered and their arguments closely scrutinized. The various arguments were found to be invalid, unsound, or at cross-purposes with Davidson's claims, and it was concluded that the three objections posed no threat to Davidson's method of event individuation.

Finally, to still suspicions voiced in the philosophical literature and perhaps also evoked by the reconsideration of the three objections, the question was considered whether the individuation dispute between unifiers and multipliers might be a trivial verbal one. After an examination of various interfaces between the two accounts this question was answered in the negative.

At this juncture, then, we are left with the unifying approach seemingly intact, while the multiplying account has proved itself mistaken, inadequate, incoherent, and poorly motivated.

The time has now come for taking stock of what has been established by this defence of Davidson's unifying approach against its main critics. In what follows I will try to connect what has been established—and also the limitations thereof—to some of the general questions concerning ontological matters that naturally arise in this area.

7.2 Some Ontological Matters

One of the consequences of a unifying position on event individuation is that counting events turns out to be very much like counting ordinary objects. Events can be described, referred to, denoted, and classified in a multiplicity of ways, identified and reidentified under a variety of descriptions, just as we do with ordinary objects. Counting events requires no special algorithms.

This is a comforting result, insofar as it simplifies our relationship to the world. It also bespeaks of an ontological similarity or common ground between the categories of objects and events. Insofar as we describe and redescribe, classify and reclassify both events and objects by means of expressions which ascribe or attribute different properties to them, events are property-bearers in much the same way as objects. This may even be a similarity that can be cashed out reductively (though I must admit I am dubious of this).

Now it might be thought that a major weakness of my Davidsonian position is that it would be rendered otiose by any kind of successful reduction performed on events. Preliminary to answering this charge, let us distinguish two kinds of reductive enterprise, as suggested by the following theses:

(A) There are no events; there are nothing but objects, properties, and times.

(B) There are events, and they are nothing but objects, properties, and times.[1]

Accordingly, the kind of reduction indicated by (A), since it eliminates events altogether, will be termed "eliminative", whereas the reduction indicated by (B), which retains events, will be termed "noneliminative".

Strictly speaking, the unifier-multiplier dispute is (inter alia) *about* events and therefore each party to the dispute presupposes events in its account. Insofar as there would be no events towards which one could adopt either a unifying or a multiplying position, such accounts are admittedly vulnerable to an eliminative account of events.[2] But to dismiss such accounts on this ground alone would be to take a narrow view of things indeed. An eliminative account per se does not completely void a unifying or a multiplying account.

Besides the elimination of events, what would be the consequences of an eliminative account of events, anyway? Although such an account might compromise some details of my presentation of the unifier-multiplier dispute, and also render the language in which that dispute and its resolution are couched somewhat tendentious, I contend that there would remain a significant core not touched by event elimination.

Suppose there were a successful eliminative account of events in favor of some other ontological categories such as objects, properties, and times. In that event, members of these categories would be descripta of what we have been misleadingly calling "*event* de-

1. The reducing categories of objects, properties, and times do not figure essentially in my general claims about reduction. The multipliers' particular reductive deployment of these categories will come under scrutiny in section 7.3.

2. Because multipliers countenance more events, they of course have more to lose.

scriptions". Where there was thought to be a seamless descript*um*, viz. an event, there will be instead three descript*a*, viz. an object, a property, and a time. These might be thought of conjointly and without prejudice as a nominalistic sum-individual;[3] in this case an individual *de dictu* or *in intellectu*, since the "summing" relation that associates the three particulars with one another would be construed as merely a *façon de parler* or a mental act. The question of how we pick out and individuate these sum-individuals in ordinary language remains, however, and mutatis mutandis the previous conclusions with respect to individuation and counting still apply.

For a noneliminative reductive account likewise favoring objects, properties, and times, similar reasoning will apply, except that our seamy descriptum would be a *de re* individual, viz. an event, built up of particulars that belong to other ontological categories and are held together by some sort of ontological tie.[4] Since exemplification is a possible candidate for the role of ontological tie, the Goldman-Kim conception of events is a prime example of noneliminative reduction. Therefore, since we are contending that such reduction does not subvert a unifying position, we must concede to Kim at least one important sense in which his claim that

---

3. See Nelson Goodman, "A World of Individuals", in *Contemporary Readings in Logical Theory*, ed. Irving M. Copi and James A Gould (New York: The MacMillan Company, 1967), or else his *The Structure of Appearance*, 3rd ed., Boston Studies in the Philosophy of Science, vol. 53. (Dordrecht-Holland: D. Reidel Publishing Co., 1977), especially chapters 2 and 7.

4. There are different ways of setting this up. One could either now regard the summing relation itself as an ontological tie, or else continue to view it as a strictly conceptual relation that here and there happens to mirror ontological relations.

there are "no irreconcilable doctrinal differences" between him and Davidson might be correct.[5]

The options for reduction so far considered, although most pertinent to the context of our multipliers' peculiar worldview, constitute a special case for which the main question happens to be whether "the whole is greater than the sum of its parts". Naturally if one has antecedant qualms about ontological commitment to the "parts"—especially to properties and times—one will want other reductive options. So let's suppose for the sake of discussion that we have a theory so thoroughly eliminative that only objects (construed broadly enough to include agents and tokens of language) remain as ontological commitments. Instead of employing (putatively) referring expressions for events or properties or times, such a theory would employ only predicates which, not being referring expressions, carry no ontological commitment.[6]

Still, I would insist that an eliminative theory must be able to generate counterparts, in its preferred idiom, for the bulk of ordinary talk that is seemingly about events; it will have to mark somehow the distinctions relevant to the truth of such talk in ordinary circumstances. And that includes the truth of judgments of sameness and difference for events, since such judgments also get made in everyday circumstances having no truck with philosophy. (Even though Anscombe first raised the question for philosophers, the question as such is not a philosophical artifact.) If these conditions on an adequate theory are valid, then again previous conclusions concerning

5. Even this concession wants careful formulation. Davidson would not buy a reductive account which assigns second rank to events. See Davidson, "The Individuation of Events", especially 226-227 <174-175>.

6. This of course assumes that Quine's Rules of Order were followed in constructing the theory. See Willard Van Orman Quine, *Word and Object* (Cambridge, Mass: The M.I.T. Press, 1960), 242-243.

individuation and counting can be expected to survive, in some form or other, the ravages of elimination.[7]

All told, the unifier-multiplier controversy transcends general questions of event reduction.[8] My defence of Davidson thus amounts to more than merely a big "if-then" with the protasis begging the existence of events. A perhaps obvious corollary of this independence of sorts of the individuation and reduction issues—but important enough to justify belaboring—is this. If there are events, how we settle questions of individuation and counting per se need not decide for us the ontological issue of whether all, some, or no events are exemplifications of properties by objects at times. The most we can expect from a resolution of such questions is some set of constraining considerations germane to the ontological issue.

7. Cf. Bruce Aune, *Reason and Action* (Dordrecht-Holland: D. Reidel Publishing Co., 1977), 44-45.

8. Nevertheless there are consequences for some reductive accounts, e.g. that of Terence Horgan, "The Case Against Events", *Philosophical Review* 87 (1978). Horgan argues that multipliers need neither singular terms for events nor a generation relation between events—all that's needed is a "generational connective" between sentences containing singular terms for objects and times only. However, since the logic of this connective is to be determined by the same sorts of intuitions that govern Goldman's conditions for generation, such an account would be inclined to at least some of the difficulties found in Goldman's account, e.g. the problem of generational asymmetry. Cf. Cindy D. Stern, "The Prospects for Elimination of Event-talk", *Philosophical Studies* 54 (1988). Stern contends that without the assumption that events exist and other assumptions about their nature, it is unlikely that justice can be done to the full range of noun phrases found in causal contexts.

7.3 The Constituents Conception of Events

The last section shows that there is some room for agreement between unifiers and multipliers on the ontological nature of events,
i.e. that unifiers, qua their position on individuation, would not be
constrained from adopting *some* conception of events as property-
exemplifications. But even so, I believe that there are independent
considerations that can be brought to bear against the specific conception advanced by our representative multipliers, Goldman and
Kim.

So far, in discussing the individuation and identification prac-
tices of these multipliers, we have not sought to question *either*
whether events always have agents or objects, properties, and times
as "constitutents" *or* whether it even makes sense at all to think of
events as being the "structured complexes" Kim and Goldman en-
visage, with objects or agents, properties, and times as constituents.
In what follows I will take up this notion of constituents. First I will
consider the question of whether events must have objects as constituents and provide prima facie considerations which indicate that
this requirement may be too restrictive. I will then conclude by raising some doubts about the intelligibility of having times as constituents of events.[9]

What exactly then is meant when we are told that an event is a
structured complex having certain constituents? Constituents are in
some sense parts or components of wholes. That much at any rate
ought to be trivially true. Perhaps slightly less trivial is some requirement that constituting items be somehow consubstantiated,

---

9. The apparent quantification over properties might also be considered an objectionable aspect of the Goldman-Kim conception. Unfortunately the issues raised by
this worry would require a treatise of their own.

coincident, or co-located with their respective wholes, rather than merely concomitant to them—if, that is, the relation of constitution is to obtain in any pertinent sense at all.

Let us begin by examining the idea that objects or agents are necessarily constituents of events. When philosophers have toyed with the idea of events which are *not* a *something*'s having or exemplifying properties, undergoing or not undergoing change, they have turned to such things as lightning and waterfalls.[10] For in contrast to something's being struck by lightning, sheer lightning does not have a constitutive object. Or so it seems.

What reason, though, do we have for believing that such things as lightning and waterfalls are in fact events? Well, lightning and waterfalls are often said to "occur", and such talk is deemed more appropriate to events than objects.[11] Furthermore waterfalls are sometimes spoken of as natural processes, which may for example cause erosion, another natural process; and of course processes and causal relata are events. I do not find such reasons conclusive, however.

Occurrence talk is often unstraightforward. "A waterfall occurred at a bend in the stream" may be understood in various ways, depending on context. With the qualification "as we hiked along the bank", it could just mean "we encountered a waterfall at a bend in

10. E.g. R.M. Martin, *Logic, Language and Metaphysics* (New York: New York University Press, 1971), 107, and P.F. Strawson, *Individuals* (London: Methuen & Co. Ltd., 1969), 46ff; and sections 1 and 2 of Willard Van Orman Quine, "Identity, ostension, and hypostasis", in *From a Logical Point of View*, 2nd ed. (New York: Harper & Row, Publishers, 1963).

11. Except in doggerel? M.J. Cresswell, "Why Objects Exist but Events Occur", *Studia Logica* 45 (1986), purports to have identified a semantic property that distinguishes events from objects; he concludes, "George III / ought never to have occurred / one can only wonder / at so grotesque a blunder." Although Cresswell's discussion is flawed and too brief to be convincing, it is thought provoking.

the stream" or "a waterfall came into view at a bend in the stream". Alternatively, with the qualification "after last night's storm", it could mean "a waterfall came into being at a bend in the stream". In neither case does the waterfall itself seem to be the occurrence or event that is being reported, although in each case, to be sure, the waterfall figures intimately in what is reported to have occurred (viz. an encounter, a coming-into-being). This doesn't establish that waterfalls couldn't also be events. But it does suggest the possibility that waterfalls are said to occur only in virtue of being associated with an occurrence.

This much seems uncontroversial: wherever and whenever there is a waterfall, there is a process of water falling, or better, a continuous succession of "water-fallings". If waterfalls eliminatively reduce to this succession of water-fallings, then a waterfall will be just a succession of events, each having a quantity of water as constituent object. If, on the other hand, waterfalls turn out to be entities ontologically distinct from water-fallings, then a better case might be made for their being objects (albeit fluid and scattered) that continuously change some of the matter of which they are composed.[12] With waterfalls thus conceived, the changing of a waterfall's matter will be a process, insofar as matter displacing matter is a process; but the waterfall itself will not be an occurring process, save in a loose or figurative sense. So on neither conception are waterfalls good candidates for the role of event sans constituent object.

Lightning I suspect is subject to treatment along similar lines. Either lightning is an object having all sorts of inner electrical processes, or it is a succession of events having configurations of elec-

---

12. According to science this is true of tables and chairs too, what with the wanderlust of subatomic particles. But whereas this is an empirical discovery about tables and chairs, a waterfall *qua waterfall* is not merely contingently related to the process of water falling.

trons as constitutive (albeit scattered) objects. So these typical examples of events purported not to have a constitutive object do not make their case.

The examples just considered can be characterized as cases whose *language* suggests events but does not seem to implicate objects. Let us now consider another kind of case, where the objects involved in the event are easy enough to find, but where worries about their status as constituents arise.

Suppose that S cuts his finger, drawing blood. There will then be an occurrence which can be suitably labelled "S's bleeding". The blood happens to be flowing from S's finger, so S is not bleeding all over. That is to say, S is bleeding insofar as his finger is.

S's bleeding is easy enough to locate; we can specify some region of S's finger, say the cut. We can also locate S by the volume he occupies. In a clear sense the region S occupies is not included in the region his bleeding occupies, so S cannot be the constituent object of S's bleeding.[13]

Has S's bleeding then *no* constituent object? That conclusion would be too quick. However, let us note that the obvious move cannot be made either. That is, we might want to say that the constitutive object here—contrary to appearance *de parler*—is not S, but some part of S's finger. Such a move would give us an object meeting minimal location requirements for the role of constituent; but making such a move requires more subtlety than is to be found in the Goldman-Kim conception of events as property-exemplifications. The notion of exemplification that we have been given does not distinguish between "S exemplifies P at t", "S has P

13. Davidson, "The Individuation of Events", 228 <175-176>, makes a similar point (though for a different purpose): "The error lies in the assumption that if an event is a change in a substance, the location of the event is the entire space occupied by the substance."

at *t*", or "*S P-verb* at *t*" (where "*P-verb*" is some ordinary verb or verb phrase which ascribes the property *P*). Thus in terms of our example, "*S* exemplifies the property of bleeding", "*S* has the property of bleeding", and "*S* is bleeding" would merely be alternative ways of reporting the same event.[14]

There is a large class of properties which, like bleeding, are such that if a part of an agent or object has them, then ipso facto that agent or object has them. If *S*'s finger bleeds, to repeat our example, then *S* bleeds. So if we want to characterize events as property-exemplifications, with the object which does the exemplifying as constituent, we cannot also allow that the simple having of a property by an object is the same as exemplifying it. Exemplification would have to be reserved for those objects that can be placed within the boundaries of the event. For our example, that comes to one being able to say of *S*, that *S* merely has the property of bleeding but does not exemplify it; whereas some part of *S* not only has the property but exemplifies it too, thereby qualifying as constituent object of the exemplification of bleeding.

Let us grant that the conceptual means for making the requisite refinements are in principle available. Then, events involving such synecdochic properties as bleeding need not on that account constitute counterexamples to the claim that events must have constituent objects. For these cases, the constituent object will be part of a greater object—an object involved in the event and typically figuring in its everyday description, but not a constituent in it. In line with these remarks, the claim we set out to examine is then

---

14. See Goldman, *A Theory of Human Action* , 10-11, and Kim, "Events as Property Exemplifications", 160-161.

better cast as the claim that objects or agents *or their parts* are necessarily constituents of events.[15]

So far, what's been said discounts the idea that constituent objects can straightforwardly be read off from event descriptions having the canonical form, but not the idea of a structured complex as such. What I wish to suggest now is that distinguishing parts from wholes as was just done is but one way of framing answers to questions asking *where* an event occurred. In answering such questions we are not limited to specifying the location of the X referred to in the event's description, "X *verb*ed (Y) at t", or the location of X's parts. Instead, we often respond with Y's location, or locations contiguous to X or Y, or some location where the *verb*ing is manifested. In illustration consider the following questions and responses:

Q: Where did Sam telephone Fred?

A1: At the drugstore. [location contiguous to Sam]

A2: In the booth. [Sam's location]

A3: At the work site. [location contiguous to Fred]

A4: In his [Fred's] office. [Fred's location]

Q: Where did George call John?

A: Over the intercom. [manifestation of the call]

15. Another worry about constituent objects is suggested by Olav Gjelsvik, "A Note on Objects and Events", *Analysis* 48 (1988). Gjelsvik contends that since there may be more than one object at the same place at the same time—e.g. the statue and the piece of bronze it's made of—even more counterintuitive multiplication of events will result on Kim's conception of events than was previously thought. This case is comparable to my bleeding example if the statue is treated as a (temporal) part of the piece of bronze.

Q: Where was it that Kennedy was shot by Oswald?

Al: In Dallas [location of both Kennedy and Oswald]

A2: In his car. [Kennedy's location]

A3: Here. From this window. [Oswald's location]

Q: Where did Oswald fire the first shot?

A: Along this trajectory. [manifestation of the firing]

Correlative to the claim occasioning these examples, such a diversity of legitimate answers makes it plain that a statement that the location of *X*'s *verb*ing is such-and-such does not necessarily tell us where *X* is at the time. All or part of him could have been there, or he could have been entirely removed from there. *X* need not be where the event described by "*X verbed*" is.[16] So we see now that the canonical-form description of an event in terms of an object et seq. does not necessarily give us that object as constituent *even in part*. It might be objected, however, that this is a problem of language, not metaphysics; it does not follow that an event need not have an object as constituent at all. Perhaps we just need to become even more subtle about specification.

---

16. Diane Francis, "Lynden Pindling's day in court", *Maclean's*, 20 June 1988, p. 9, relates a recent judicial decision against NBC that nicely illustrates this point. The network's Canadian lawyers had filed a motion to have a libel case dropped on the grounds that it should not be heard in Canada. The presiding judge dismissed the motion, reasoning that no matter how the airwaves were beamed into Canadian living rooms, the alleged libel had also been committed in Canada, and that Canadian libel laws applied. Although highly ironic, this is otherwise not really as extraordinary as it first sounds. In fact historical events are routinely characterized in terms of things done by absent individuals. During Patton's historic fight with von Rundstedt, for example, neither officer was actually present where the fighting occurred.

Such a response is of course adequate only if there is no reason to believe that suitable candidates for constituent objects are not to be found where the event is. As we saw for the lightning and waterfall examples, just because such candidates aren't always immediately obvious, it does not mean that there are none. For one of the above cases in which Sam is not located with his *verb*ing, Fred could be constituent in his stead. For another, we might have to consider the intercom in that role. For yet another—and this may be stretching things—we may have to countenance the bullet that describes the trajectory as a possibility.

I would venture that there will be many cases (such as the last?) where the only candidates for constituent object will be perverse or contrived enough to render them suspect. However, my argument against constituent objects will not be made merely on such a basis. I will argue that there are cases where the only possible candidates for exemplifier of properties will—in contrast to Fred, the intercom, and the bullet—not be anything that falls within the categories of objects or agents at all.

Let us consider some system of heavenly bodies having a certain mass and bearing a certain spatial relationship to one another. If science is to be believed, such a system of bodies will give us the phenomenon of gravity. Now consider what will be the case when an object is placed in space between two propinquitous bodies in such a system. Depending on how it is placed it will be drawn towards one rather than the other, or neither, if the gravitational pull exerted by the bodies happens to be equal.

There is a sense in which a force exerted on an object will "involve" the bodies which exert that force no matter where those bodies are in relation to the manifestation of the exerted force. Suppose, however, we are concerned only with what happens in the region where the object between the two bodies is located, some region small enough to exclude those bodies. Clearly the bodies are exerting force and are exerting it in, among other places, that region. But although what happens in that region is evidently dependent on the existence of these bodies and on their being related in certain ways to that region, in a clear sense they are not constituents of any event occurring in that region, since for one thing they are not even there. If the constituents of a thing are not where the thing is, the term "constituent" is not very helpful. It may be objected that the constitutive object in this case is not either of the heavenly bodies, but the object between them. It is this object that exemplifies the property of having force exerted on it by the two bodies, and it is therefore the constitutent object of what is happening in the region where it is located.

I would now claim that if that object were eliminated from the picture, the two heavenly bodies would still be exerting force in a place where they are not. Here some might object that gravity cashes out as action at a distance, not through a distance. Where there are no objects, nothing happens in terms of gravitational force. However, since it is at least an open question in physics whether gravitation can be subsumed under more general features of the underlying quantum field, that response begs the question.[17] Also, there are similar examples that perhaps aren't quite as controversial. One such would be the generation of magnetic fields, which are typically thought of as spread homogeneously over a region irrespective of objects therein. (Again, it is at least an open question whether magnetic and gravitational forces can be conflated in a unified field theory.) Insofar as examples like these involve empirical assumptions, they describe possible cases, even if those assumptions end up dis-

17. See Daniel Z. Freedman and Peter von Nieuwenhuizen, "Supergravity and the Unification of the Laws of Physics", *Scientific American* 238 (February 1978).

confirmed or proven false. That such cases are possible would have the consequence, other things being equal, that it is not necessary that every event have a constituent object.

As a last resort, those who would resist this conclusion might choose to argue that other things are not equal because some candidates for constituent object have been overlooked. As far as I can see, though, the room to manoeuvre here is limited.

Vacuums might be thought to qualify as objects which exemplify magnetic or gravitational properties, but that would have to be reconciled with the standard characterization of vacuums as being regions devoid of objects.[18] Fields also might be thought of as objects, but this has to be reconciled with the fact that vacuums preempt objects but not fields; also, fields can pass through objects in a way objects cannot pass through objects.

In these respects forces would fare much the same as fields. But forces would be even more unpalatable as constituent object for quite another reason. Suppose we did seriously reify force to serve as constituent object in the gravitational example. Then we would have the force exemplifying—what? The property of exerting force? Strictly speaking, I should think that forces do not exert force—they simply have a magnitude.[19] So in reifying force we do not seem to get a suitable exemplifier for the property in question.

18. Cf. the introductory remarks of Lewis P. Fulcher, Johann Rafelski, and Abraham Klein, "The Decay of the Vacuum", *Scientific American* 241 (December, 1979).

19. Some remarks of Nietzsche's are quite apropos here: 'The popular mind in fact doubles the deed; when it sees the lightning flash, it is the deed of a deed: it posits the same event first as cause and then a second time as its effect. Scientists do no better when they say "force moves", "force causes", and the like—all its coolness, its freedom from emotion notwithstanding, our entire science still lies under the misleading influence of language....'—From essay 1, section 13 of *On the Genealogy of Morals,* trans. Walter Kaufmann and R.J. Hollingdale, in *On the Genealogy of Morals and Ecce Homo,* ed. Walter Kaufmann (New York: Vintage Books, 1967).

I would suggest that forces have more in common with things like walks, hangings, murders, etc.—which are also denoted by expressions which do double-duty as nouns and verbs—than they have in common with objects or agents. Just as we would not expect the nominalization of the *verb* "man" to denote men but rather something men do, so we ought not to expect that the nominalization of the verb "force" denotes something that exerts force, rather than something done by things that exert force.

If the parallel I am suggesting is correct, then seeking constituent objects in kinds of things like forces is misguided, for these are not of the right ontological category for filling that role. They are not objects but events. This conclusion comports with, and ceteris paribus draws some further support from, the fact that we often speak of forces as occurrences and as causal relata.

In the light of the foregoing discussion, it appears that there can be events without constituent objects, and that therefore the Goldman-Kim conception of events is not sufficiently general.

Let us now turn to the question of whether events must—or even can—have times as constituents. Events occur at or during times. In this loose sense, events can be said to "involve" times. But why should the fact that every event requires a time for it to occur entail that times are constituents of events?

Constituents and the wholes of which they are constituents, as I ventured above, are not merely concomitants. In the nonsupernatural realm, I should think this means that constituents exist at at least some of the times at which the things they are constituents of exist. In this case the things the alleged constituents are allegedly constituents of, viz. events, are things that exist only when they occur. Events occur at times. Therefore, if times are constituents of events, times exist at times. I find this conclusion unintelligible and take it to yield a *reductio* of the assumption that times are constituents of events.

It might be objected that there is another way of looking at the situation which has the sanction of philosophical tradition. Metaphysicians and logicians sometimes speak of a mode of existence called "timeless existence". Facts, numbers, and the like are often said to exist in this way; properties too are sometimes said to exist timelessly, independent of whether anything for a time has them. The nature of these things is such that it is somehow inappropriate to speak of them as existing for definite periods of time. Times fall into this category and therefore may be spoken of as having timeless existence. So there is a sense in which we may assert both that the exemplification of a property by an object at a time exists, and that this existent has a time as constituent.

This indeed is intelligible, but only goes to support my previous conclusion. The existent here is one which exists timelessly and so cannot be an event. Events are datable entities.

In essence these two approaches to the question could be presented in the form of a simple constructive dilemma. Either a property-exemplification with a time as constituent occurs at a time or it doesn't. In the former case, it cannot be an event, because events can intelligibly be said to exist at times. In the latter case, it cannot be an event, because events do not exist timelessly. So a property-exemplification with a time as constituent cannot be an event.

Let me now conclude with a few remarks on the approach I have taken with respect to constituents. In tackling the notion of constituents, a central concern is that some means be provided for separating things concomitant to or merely involved vis-à-vis some entity from things which are truly constituents of that entity. Married men have wives, and in that sense the existence of a married man can be said to involve the existence of a wife. Yet I take it we would not want to make the claim that every married man has a wife as constituent. So we must have a notion of constituent which does not allow such moves. I suggested and employed spatiotemporal co-location of constituents with what they constitute as a minimal condition on such a notion, partly because it does bar such moves and partly because of its intuitive appeal. This condition then enabled me to argue that it is neither the case that events need have objects as constituents, nor the case that events can have times as constituents.

It can, of course, be claimed that I am just being obtuse and have failed to grasp the notion of constituent at issue here. But in that case, the notion or metaphor is not an obvious one and requires unpacking by those who would embrace it.

While this may not be the final word on the matter, it clearly puts the ball in the other court. As things stand at present it appears that even though it is open for unifiers to adopt some conception of events as property-exemplifications, the Goldman-Kim constituents conception is not an acceptable candidate.

8

THE CAUSAL CRITERION OF EVENT IDENTITY

8.1 Preamble

Except for brief mention in chapter 2 in the course of presenting the causal objection to Davidson's identity claims, nothing has been said so far about Davidson's criterion of event identity. The main reason for this is that at the level at which the discussion proceeded, the criterion as such was not needed for purposes of pressing the particular claims under debate. The arguments pro and con turned for the most part on other considerations.

This is of course in marked contrast to the role played by the multipliers' criterion of event identity in the discussion. But then from the multipliers' point of view the situation was also markedly different. In denying Davidson's explanatory identities they needed to replace them with a new explanatory relation, and their criterion figured essentially in their account of that relation.

My decision to bring up Davidson's criterion at this point—in addition to an aesthetic concern for symmetry in the treatment of unifiers and multipliers—is motivated by a consequence of the ontological discussion of the preceding chapter. In undermining the multipliers' constituents conception of events, we have in effect also undermined their criterion of event identity, since their criterion presupposes that conception of events. A concern that naturally arises in the light of this consequence is whether some alternative criterion is available. In the present context, it is fitting that we ask whether the criterion proposed by our representative unifier might be adequate to the task. That question will be the main concern of this chapter.

In what follows I will consider various charges of inadequacy that have been levelled against Davidson's criterion and determine the seriousness of these charges. The discussion of adequacy will have two parts. First, we will consider charges to the effect that the criterion is (loosely speaking) uninteresting or trivial in some sense. Then we will consider the question of its truth or correctness.

A discussion of how the criterion relates to matters of individuation will be left to the remaining chapter.

8.2 Is Davidson's Criterion Interesting?

Davidson's criterion of event identity, it will be recalled, is a causal criterion. It states that events are identical if and only if they have exactly the same causes and effects,[1] or more formally,

$$x=y \quad \text{if and only if} \quad [(\forall z) (z \text{ caused } x \to z \text{ caused } y) \, \&$$
$$(\forall z) (x \text{ caused } z \to y \text{ caused } z)],$$

where x and y are events.

---

1. Davidson, "The Individuation of Events", 231 <179>.

Possibly in anticipation of criticism, Davidson adds that while the criterion "seems to have an air of circularity about it", it is not formally circular since no identities appear on the right-hand side of the biconditional. However, many nonetheless feel that this does not save the criterion from being circular in a damaging way.

As a point of departure, we will begin by examining the view that the criterion is inadequate because circular. While I myself have been a proponent of this view,[2] I now believe that it is based on certain confusions and non sequiturs. This has been established in a paper by Bernard D. Katz.[3] I will first cite the arguments purporting to show that Davidson's criterion is circular and then present Katz's counterarguments. The imputations of circularity fall into two categories. The first kind questions the usability of such a criterion in passing judgment on event identity. Thus we find Munroe Beardsley saying that

> there seems to be a kind of implicit pragmatic circularity (or circularity of application) in [Davidson's criterion]—apart from the threat of an infinite regress in application. Thus suppose we are to decide whether e and f are the same event, and we know that e caused g and f caused h. We must first decide whether their effects are the same, that is, whether $g = h$. But to decide this, we must first decide whether the causes of g and h are the same, namely whether $e = f$. To give an example, suppose the alarm clock's ringing woke Susan up one morning; but suppose it was the loudness of that ringing that brought her suddenly wide awake. We want to know whether
>
> (46) the alarm's ringing = the alarm's ringing loudly
> so we have to decide first whether

---

2. Karl Pfeifer, "Davidson's Criterion of Event Identity", read at the Seminar on Science and Philosophy, Interuniverzitetski Centar za Postdiplomski Studij, Dubrovnik, 5 April 1979. Dagfinn Føllesdal's friendly but devastating criticism set me straight.

3. Bernard D. Katz, "Is the Causal Criterion of Event-Identity Circular?", *Australasian Journal of Philosophy* 56 (1978).

(47) Susan's awakening = Susan's wide awakening
—and vice versa.[4]

Similarly, we find Myles Brand saying that the criterion involves an informal "epistemological" circularity which

> counts against using [Davidson's criterion] as a criterion for individuation, that is, a criterion for *judging* whether *e* and *f* are identical. As Davidson has rightly emphasized, the relata of the causal relation are events. Now one event causes another only if they are distinct (that is, nonidentical), at least according to the ordinary notion of causation. By [Davidson's criterion], *e* and *f* are distinct only if there is some event causally related to *e* but not *f*, or conversely. Hence, it cannot be correctly judged whether the definiens is satisfied without first knowing whether the definiendum is satisfied *and conversely.*[5]

The second kind of informal circularity is supposedly of a logical nature. Regarding this circularity Brand says,

> The definiens of [Davidson's criterion] requires quantification over events. But quantification over events in the definiens is permissible only if there is an identity criterion independent of [Davidson's criterion].[6]

These, then, are the arguments behind the allegations of circularity. Let me now sketch Katz's very compelling reasoning against these charges.

Katz states that in general, a criterion for the identity of ∅'s presupposes that we can determine that certain predicates are true of individual ∅'s. He acknowledges, in particular, that the adequacy of

---

4. Beardsley, "Actions and Events: The Problem of Individuation", 271.

5. Myles Brand, "Particulars, Events, and Actions" in *Action Theory*, ed. M. Brand and D. Walton (Dordrecht-Holland: D. Reidel Publishing Co., 1976), 138.

6. Brand, "Particulars, Events, and Actions", 138.

the causal criterion as a criterion for event identity presupposes that we can determine when individual events are related as cause and effect. A further condition of adequacy for the criterion is that we should in principle be able to establish that events have the same causes and effects without first establishing that those events are the same.

As the quotation above makes evident, Brand charges that the criterion is epistemologically circular because the last condition is not met. His reasons are (i) if one event follows another, they are not identical, and (ii) given Davidson's criterion, if events are not identical they do not have the same causes and effects. However, what follows from (i) and (ii), Katz argues, is only that if events have the same causes and effects they are not related as cause and effect, and not Brand's conclusion that we cannot know that events have the same causes and effects without first knowing that they are identical. To get that conclusion, two further assumptions are needed, viz. (iii) that we cannot know that events have the same causes and effects without first establishing that they are not related as cause and effect (doubted but granted by Katz) and (iv) that we cannot establish that events are not related as cause and effect without first establishing that they are identical. However (iv) is mistaken since it is obvious that two events can fail to be causally related without thereby being one. Thus Katz disposes of Brand's objection.

Katz also has an argument which, though not specifically addressed to it, is germane to Beardsley's charge of "pragmatic" circularity. Having successfully defended the assumption that it can be determined that a pair of events have the same causes and effects independently of determining that the events in question are identical, Katz now turns to consider the contention that what is stated in the assumption could not be done without prior familiarity with other event identities. If so, and those other event identities could not be established without recourse to the causal criterion, then (prima facie) there would be a vicious circle (this is more or less Beardsley's point reworded).

Katz goes on to argue that this objection rests on a mistaken assumption. Admittedly, to establish that events have the same causes and effects we must suppose events exist and that there are criteria for their identity. But, he insists, it is a mistake to suppose that in order to show that events have the same causes and effects, we must apply those criteria to other events and first establish other event identities.

He reinforces this claim with the following reasoning. Consider a partial instantiation of the first conjunct of the definiens of Davidson's criterion, viz. "$(\forall z)$ (z caused $e \longleftrightarrow z$ caused f)"[7] where "e" and "f" are singular terms for events. We must show that the open sentence which remains after the quantifier is deleted is true under every assignment of events to its free variables. Katz acknowledges that this requires causal knowledge, since in order to evaluate the result of each assignment we must have information about the extension of "caused" that enables us to establish whether certain ordered pairs of events satisfy "x caused y". However, Katz continues, this does not require that we be able to determine whether certain events are the same or different.

Katz concludes:

---

7. Strictly speaking this is not the first conjunct of the "definiens" of the causal criterion as stated by Davidson himself. However, since we know identity to be symmetric, a test for $e=f$ is also a test for $f=e$ and "$(\forall z)$ (z caused $e \longrightarrow z$ caused f)" will be true if and only if "$(\forall z)$ (z caused $f \longrightarrow z$ caused e)" is true. Thus it is of no consequence whether a conditional or a biconditional is employed in stating the criterion. I make this point because J.E. Tiles (see n. 11 below) seems to see a problem here.

The assumption concerning causal knowledge may be thought problematic for one reason or another, but there is no reason to suppose that such information *must* involve, or presuppose, knowledge of event-identities. Accordingly, there is no *theoretical* reason to suppose that we could not establish that events are causally coincident [i.e. have the same causes and effects] without first establishing that they, or any other events, are identical.[8]

Thus Katz takes himself to have dispatched the charge of epistemological circularity against Davidson's criterion. I find his reasoning incontrovertible. Katz also has some illuminating remarks in objection to the charge of "logical" circularity, but for present purposes it is not necessary to recapitulate those here.[9] There is a shortcut we can take vis-à-vis that charge: the demand that a statement of conditions of identity not quantify over those entities whose conditions of identity are being specified is not one we make in other contexts. For example, the principle of extensionality for sets, viz. that sets are identical just in case they have exactly the same members, does not restrict membership to nonsets. So the demand as stated is not one which needs to be respected.

There may of course remain worries that are not touched by Katz's defense of the criterion or not captured by the notion of circularity. Such worries are suggested by the fact that the complaints about circularity are accompanied by remarks which indicate that other desiderata, perhaps separable from the desideratum of noncircularity, are at stake. These desiderata are expressed in terms of

8. Katz, "Is the Causal Criterion of Event-Identity Circular?", 228-229.

9. Katz, "Is the Causal Criterion of Event-Identity Circular?", 228-229.

such notions as "getting clear about entities",[10] "usability",[11] "usefulness", and "informativeness".[12]

I am not prepared to examine in detail how Davidson's criterion fares with respect to these notions. Because of their vague and equivocal nature that task would simply be too great an undertaking in the present context. Suffice it to say, preanalytically and equally vaguely, that these notions seem to be "purpose-relative". That is, Davidson's criterion may be useful for certain purposes but not others, informative for or with respect to certain purposes but not others, etc. The purposes the critics have in mind are not made manifest, and, furthermore, may not be the same as Davidson's. In the latter case criticism based on the critics' concerns could be viewed as irrelevant. The (often tacit) concern to achieve an ontological reduction, for example, might just be one such irrelevant concern.

Naturally, if one requires that a criterion be reductive in order, say, to be informative, one will find Davidson's criterion uninformative. However, that kind of demand would be an unreasonable one to make. It is simply false that a criterion has to yield the sort of information given by a reductive criterion in order to be at all informative. Again, the principle of extensionality for sets provides a case in point. It is not reductive, but nonetheless worth stating.

Whether satisfying such demands is a desideratum ultimately to be met is of course a question that deserves consideration and is likely to be answered in the affirmative. However, the fact that such demands have not been met does not detract from the importance of more limited gains. It is of course possible that our detractors might

10. N.L. Wilson, "Facts, Events and Their Identity Conditions", *Philosophical Studies* 25 (1974), 303-304.

11. J.E. Tiles, "Davidson's Criterion of Event Identity", *Analysis* 36 (1976), 185.

12. Brand, "Particulars, Events, and Actions", 136ff.

accept these remarks and yet press the criticism, insisting that nothing has been gained. To preempt that move, let me adduce some evidence to the contrary.

One respect in which Davidson's criterion is both interesting and informative is suggested by the fact, which may not have gone unnoticed, that the criterion is as good as an instantiation of a schema presented by Willard Van Orman Quine as a recipe for defining "identity" in a logical theory having some two-place predicate, "ø", as its only primitive.[13]

For such a theory, Quine says, "=" may be defined adequately by explaining "$x = y$" as

$$(\forall z) \; [(\emptyset xz \longleftrightarrow \emptyset yz) \; \& \; (\emptyset zx \longleftrightarrow \emptyset zy)]$$

This schema would preserve the laws of identity given by "$x=x$" and all instances of the schema "$(x=y \; \& \; Fx) \to Fy$".[14]

Quine goes on to say that the sense of "$x = y$" given by his plan for definition may or may not really be identity, this depending on the predicate chosen to instantiate "ø" and the domain of quantification. For example, if the domain is that of persons and the predicate replacing "ø" ascribes a comparison of their incomes, then obviously this manner of defining "$x = y$" will equate any persons having the same income. "In cases of this kind," Quine remarks,

> we could protest that the interpretation of the universe and predicates is ill chosen, and that it might better be so rectified as to construe the

13. Willard Van Orman Quine, *Set Theory and Its Logic*, rev. ed. (Cambridge, Massachusetts: The Belknap Press of Harvard University Press, 1969), 13.

14. Quine provides a proof. Note that schemata such as "Fx" and "Fy" may represent sentences of any degree of complexity; the dummy letters "F" and "G" need not stand for simple explicit predicates.

members of the universe as whole income groups. But even at worst, even if we do not thus rectify the interpretation in order to sustain our method of defining '$x = y$', still no discrepancies between it and genuine identity can be registered in terms of the vocabulary of the theory itself. Even in the perverse case, thus, the method defines something as good as identity for purposes of the theory concerned.[15]

What can we say about Davidson's criterion, against such a Quineian backdrop, that would give it some interest? With a little embroidery, maybe something like this. The criterion may be construed as expressing the claim that, for a domain of events, the simple causal predicate is perhaps unique among English predicates in that it can be consistently relied on to yield genuine identities in a theory where the identity sign is introduced by means of Quine's recipe. Understood in this light, Davidson's criterion certainly embodies an interesting and, if true, informative claim.

15. Quine, *Set Theory and Its Logic*, 15.

8.3 Is Davidson's Criterion True?

Now let us turn to the crucial question, viz. whether or not the causal criterion is true in addition to being interesting. Before taking up objections gleaned from the literature, let me present a kind of example which to my knowledge has not been raised in objection to Davidson. We can dub this anticipatory objection the "cosmological" objection since what my example suggests is that, prima facie, Davidson's criterion does not sit well with certain cosmological theories currently espoused by segments of the scientific community.

Let us suppose that the physical universe has a finite history. There is a definite coming into being, perhaps a "big bang", and a last event after which there is nothing. The entire history of the universe may be taken as a big event. Now consider any continuous sequence of subevents entirely synchronous with this big event, say the history of a particle which exists as part of the universe from beginning to end. Let us consider these two events, the history of the universe and the history of the particle. Since there are no events, preceding or following these events, which could stand in causal relations to them, they would seem to satisfy the definiens of Davidson's criterion by default. But since these events are not in fact identical, the stated identity conditions cannot be sufficient.

This example suggests either that Davidson's criterion requires a cosmology that does not have *both* first and last events,[16] or (what may not be importantly different here) that it requires a linguistic framework not amenable to certain kinds of talk. Either way, though, Davidson's criterion appears to be in trouble.

16. "Neither first nor last events" would be too strong here. A universe temporally bounded on one end only would trivially satisfy only one of the conjuncts in the definiens of the criterion. Differentiation could still be accomplished by means of the other disjunct. This point will come up again shortly.

In the former case, such a cosmology is just not built into the notion of an event or a cause—it embodies claims having empirical content which are not to be settled by merely reflecting on these notions. In the latter case, the very existence of cosmological theories with competing claims vis-à-vis beginnings and endings of the universe, first causes, etc. appears to indicate that such talk is intelligible.

Of course it may just be that such talk is too crude, and therefore misleading if taken at face value. Perhaps more subtlety in the form of certain qualifications is required. For example, even though we can intelligibly use the word "event" for each, it might just be that events spanning the history of the universe ought not to be viewed in the same light as events spanning a proper part within that history; likewise for events involving ultimate beginnings and endings.

Regrettably I have little to say at present on this question of according special status to certain events in order to place them beyond the reach of the criterion. I merely point it out as *a* possible and not unprecedented way to go, assuming appropriate motivation can be supplied.[17] The apprehension that ultimate beginnings, endings, and all-encompassing events differ dramatically from ordinary day-to-day events might be a start in that direction.

Be that as it may, since the need for special status is at least an open question, the cosmological objection to Davidson's criterion falls short of being conclusive. Admittedly this conclusion is wishy-washy. However, it will emerge from the following example that the

---

17. Compare this with the situation in set theory, where for various reasons we tell special stories about the null set, both to distinguish it from other sets and from other memberless entities.

problem need not be pursued in this way after all, thus rendering the question academic.

Even if we could exorcise the cosmological problem by the appropriate incantations, a similar problem seems to occur with more ordinary events. All we have to do, it is claimed, is imagine such events as having neither causes nor effects,[18] i.e. as being "causally isolated". Such events would be wrongly identified with each other by the criterion on the same grounds as the cosmic-scale events of the last example. And such events do not seem to be precluded by the notion of an event either.

I will dub this newly raised objection the "isolational" objection. That the cosmological objection, suitably framed, can be subsumed under the isolational objection as a special case I will assume requires no argument. Any considerations that are effective in defusing the isolational objection will also defuse the cosmological objection, and in so doing undercut the move previously contemplated against the cosmological objection. Let us then move on to see what can be accomplished in this regard.

There may be good independent reasons for maintaining that every event has a cause, say as a presupposition of scientific method.[19] However, even in that quarter it has not gone unassailed. The advocates of spontaneous biological generation, whose claims were neither unintelligible nor unreasonable, provide a case in point. Likewise in physics there is sometimes talk of particles which do not interact with any other particles and then go on to suffer "spontaneous annihilation".

18. Brand, "Particulars, Events, and Actions", 137.

19. Ernst Mach appears to have held the view that the notion of cause in science gets its content from the methodology of science (the mathematical component in particular) in a way that guarantees every event's having a cause. See Mario Bunge, *Causality,* 3rd ed. (New York: Dover Publications, Inc., 1979), 90-92.

Consider then the simple case of the brief existence of a spontaneously "created" then "annihilated" particle which in the interlude does not interact with any other particle. Does it follow that an event so described has *neither* causes *nor* effects? I think not.

I will not dispute the possibility that such an event is uncaused.[20] In order to meet the current objection it is sufficient that *one* of the conjuncts in the definiens of the criterion not be trivially satisfied. Although two events might have the same causes in the logician's sense—by virtue of having no causes at all—they could still be differentiated on Davidson's criterion in terms of their effects. I make this explicit because some philosophers mistakenly suppose that Davidson's criterion depends on universal causal determinism for its truth.[21] This is not so. What it does depend on is the *disjunctive* thesis that every event either have or be a cause.

So I will respond instead to the contention that the particle example is an example of an event with no effects. I believe this can be resisted. The very existence of an event seems to me to have some minimal but unavoidable causal characteristics.

In the case of the particle, for example, there are such unavoidable effects as the vacuum's being kept at bay or displaced by the particle involved in the event. Indeed, the very extension of an object may be thought of as described by the force field it generates—and of course "generate" and "force" are causal verbs.

---

20. Although certain conditions are required for so-called spontaneous so-called creation to occur, that, ceteris paribus, is not the same as a causal connection—in some idiolects, at any rate. Such underlying conditions do not guarantee a spontaneous creation but only raise the probability of one occurring.

21. E.g. Brand, "Particulars, Events, and Actions", 137; Kim, "Events as Property Exemplification", 164.

We might think here in terms of an analogy with ordinary everyday objects. An object's surface is where its field ends or drops below threshold values. The catastrophic effects of vacuums on organismic objects are well known; an organism can maintain its surface integrity only briefly before exploding and dying.[22] An elementary particle, being elementary, can't explode of course. But its survival in the face of possible total annihilation also depends on its maintaining (actively or passively) some sort of equilibrium with its milieu. Successive states of an object or particle are comparably causally dependent on one another, later stages being dependent on earlier ones. The very existence of contingent entities requires exercise of causal powers. For objects, "to be is to do". *For events, to be is to be a cause.*

One counterobjection that might be raised against this attempt to defend Davidson's criterion against the isolational objection is that what I am suggesting violates the commonplace that "causes precede their effects". This can of course be understood in a number of ways. One thing this commonplace suggests—which is perhaps *the* grain of truth in it—is that there is a "direction" of causal necessitation between causal relata which shares certain topological features with the temporal orderings between them. My reasoning above is compatible with such a suggestion, provided it is not taken to rule out the possibility of causes or parts of causes being contemporaneous with their effects.

Now the denial, whether implicit or explicit, of such a possibility by some philosophers is perhaps attributable to preoccupation with the paradigm of causation epitomized by billiard ball colli-

---

22. This was graphically represented in the movie *Outland,* dir. Peter Hyams, (U.S.A., 1981).

sions.[23] However a lot of causation is just not like that—as a little reflection on mundane examples quickly makes plain. Consider, for instance, a locomotive pulling a caboose. The motion of the locomotion is causing the motion of the caboose, but they are moving in unison nonetheless.[24] So the anticipated counterobjection, if it doesn't simply misjudge the innocuous truth I've already conceded, presumes a false generalization about causation.

If what I have been contending is correct, then events—with the one exception below—will have intrinsic causal efficacy; their mere occurrence will have unavoidable side effects. Furthermore, this applies as well to the kinds of events we considered in the cosmological objection. Events which span the history of the universe can have contemporaneous side effects, in terms of which they can be differentiated right to the bitter end. The one exception would be that event comprising everything that happens in the universe's history. But then there is at most one such event in any case. So trivial satisfaction of the condition expressed in the definiens of Davidson's criterion will not result in incorrect identifications.

23. Even in cases that do fit the collision paradigm there may be a sort of simultaneity involving some causes and effects. When one billiard ball hits another, for example, an event involving the first ball ends and an event involving the second ball begins. If there is no temporal interval between these two events, the second follows the first without delay. In this sense the end of the first event is simultaneous with the onset of the second. Such interfacial simultaneity is depicted by cases (ii), (iii), and (v) in section 5.5 above. It should also be noted that this simultaneity does not depend on actual contact of the balls, as long as there is action at a (very small) distance. I mention this because contact, strictly conceived, might be thought impossible; for in Cartesian space there is no middle ground between being separated and being merged.

24. This example is discussed by Richard Taylor, "Causation", in *The Encyclopedia of Philosophy*, reprint edition, ed. Paul Edwards (New York: Macmillan Publishing Co., Inc. & The Free Press, 1972), vol. 2, 64-65.

In considering and rejecting the isolational objection, we have killed two birds with one stone. That is, we have thereby also found a way of undermining the cosmological objection independently of according special status to certain kinds of events, as was initially suggested. However the case against Davidson's criterion does not rest entirely on the possibility of uncaused or ineffectual events. A very novel challenge to Davidson's criterion has come from Judith Jarvis Thomson. Her purported counterexample does not rely on any denial of causal interactions in a particular case; instead, it capitalizes on the consideration that events have other events as parts. Let us examine Thomson's objection to the criterion.

In making her case, Thomson invites us to consider a complex event, her vacuuming of the carpets, which has as parts the following causal sequence of events: her pressing the button, the electrical circuit's closing, the motor's starting, and the air's starting to be sucked through the hose. We are also asked to consider an event, Alpha, composed of all the parts of the vacuuming with the exception of the circuit's closing. Thomson comments on these two events as follows:

> Alpha is discrete from the electrical circuit's closing and hence is not identical with my vacuuming of those carpets. Yet I should imagine that Alpha and my vacuuming of the carpets have exactly the same causes, and exactly the same effects. They plainly have the same causes. And they have the same effects if it can be supposed that not only does the electrical circuit's closing cause something in Alpha, but so also does every event that is part of the circuit's closing cause something in Alpha—if every part of it causes something in Alpha, then, by (IV), Alpha causes no part of it.... the fact that there are—and I think there is no good reason not to allow that there are—events such as Alpha shows [Davidson's criterion] to be false.[25]

25. Thomson, *Acts and Other Events*, 70. "(IV)" in the quoted passage designates Thomson's principle that E is caused by y if and only if there is an x such that x is

What Thomson has done is describe two events, the vacuuming and Alpha, which (she claims) have the same causes and effects even though they are nonidentical. Clearly if Alpha were not a possible event, Thomson would have no counterexample to Davidson's criterion. This fact might induce those whose sympathies lie with Davidson to regard with suspicion events such as Alpha, composed as they are of spatiotemporally scattered parts.[26] I believe, however, that such doubt about the legitimacy of events like Alpha would be misplaced in the present context. So I will try to bring to bear a different direction.

Thomson's example is a counterexample to Davidson only if a very special assumption (A), which is not made explicit in the quoted passage, is granted. Below I will first argue that (A) is false. Then I will go on to show that when (A) is replaced by a more plausible variant (A*), Thomson's example is not after all a counterexample to Davidson's criterion.

To this end, I will focus on the claim that the vacuuming and Alpha have exactly the same causes. Unfortunately, Thomson has not made her reasoning plain here. One possible line of support, though, might be drawn from two quite reasonable suppositions. These are the supposition that whatever causes all the parts of the vacuuming causes all the parts of Alpha (because Alpha is included in the vacuuming) and the supposition that whatever causes all the

---

part of y, and x causes E, and no part of E is part of y, and no part of E causes part of y (p. 66); the variables are taken to range over events. This principle will not figure in my discussion below.

26. Indeed, just that sort of response may be found in Stephen P. Schwartz, Review of *Acts and Other Events*, by Judith Jarvis Thomson, *Philosophical Review* 88 (1979), 102, 104.

parts of Alpha could conceivably cause all the parts of the vacuuming.[27] However, these suppositions alone would not be sufficient to force the conclusion that Davidson's criterion is false. For that we also need as premise the assumption (A), that the only causes an event has are those which cause every one of its parts.

(A) is indeed available to Thomson as a premise, since it is entailed by her explicit assumption that C causes y if and only if C causes all of y's parts.[28] It is (A)—and hence also this assumption that entails (A)—that I find more suspicious than events like Alpha in this context.

Let us consider some examples that appear to support this suspicion. Take the example of a postmortem diagnosis of the causes of the terrible performance of a certain play. We would surely not wish to exclude the consumption of contaminated food by the actors during intermission merely on the grounds that this did not have any effect with respect to the preintermission parts of the performance. This fact shows (A) to be untenable.

Consider as well the example of a boxer who, at the end of round 10, has his face in a rather sorry state. One might inquire as to what made his face look like *that* and get as answer that it was the hook in round 7, the jab in round 8, and the slash in round 9. Such an answer might be appropriate for a latecomer to the fight. Alternatively, one could also get as answer simply that it was the slash in round 9. Such an answer might be appropriate for someone who missed that particular blow. Given the blows suffered in previous rounds, that slash was all that was required to get his face into that condition—to bring out its color, so to speak.

27. See Schwartz, Review of *Acts and Other Events*, 102.

28. Thomson, *Acts and Other Events*, 63.

Compare the last example to the proverbial striking of the match. I may get the match to light by *rubbing it dry between my palms and then striking it*—or, having rubbed it dry, I may then get it to light by *striking it*. The fact that the latter cause is in a sense only partial does not tell against its being a cause. Similarly, it would seem, the fact that the individual punches make their own unique contributions to the mess that is the boxer's face ought not to tell against the last punch's being a cause of that mess. If so, this again indicates that (A) is untenable.

That (A) is untenable is in itself enough to undermine Thomson's reasoning as I have reconstructed it. But we can go further. If we replace (A) with (A*) below, we will be able to show that Thomson's example is not a counterexample to Davidson. (A*), a plausible alternative to (A), may be abstracted from the above examples. (A*) would state that it is sufficient for an event to be counted among the causes of another event if it is a cause of some of the parts of that event but is not itself a part of that event.[29]

Given (A*), the existence of an event such as Alpha can be seen to be compatible with Davidson's criterion in the following way. Ex hypothesi the vacuuming and Alpha share all the causes which precede the pressing of the button and all the effects which follow the air's starting to be sucked up through the hose. The electrical circuit's closing causes what is both a part of the vacuuming and of Alpha, viz. the motor's starting and the air's being sucked through the hose. Since the electric circuit's closing is part of the vacuuming, it cannot be a cause of the vacuuming. However, it is not a part of

---

29. The qualification expressed in the second conjunct is needed to rule out an event's being a cause of itself.

Alpha, and would, if (A*) is correct, be a cause of Alpha.[30] By Davidson's criterion the vacuuming and Alpha would therefore be distinct since Alpha has a cause that the vacuuming lacks.[31] So we see that once (A) is discarded, events such as Alpha do not invalidate Davidson's criterion of event identity.

Has Thomson a way of responding to this? Well, she might insist that partial causes "by definition" cause only part of the caused event, so of course the principle that C causes y if and only if C causes all of y's parts does not hold for partial causes of the caused event; it only holds for unqualified causes of that event and these are what is at issue.[32] But the only backing Thomson provides for this principle is the answer-begging rhetorical question "For how could an event C cause an event y without causing everything that y con-

30. Cf. the following causal claim made by Allan Bloom in *The Closing of the American Mind* (New York: Touchstone Books/Simon and Schuster, Inc., 1988), 346. Writing of the crisis of liberal education, Bloom says that "a large part of the story is just the general debilitation of the humanities, which is both symptom and cause of our present condition." Keeping in mind that a symptom is just a fancy kind of effect, read "Alpha" for "our present condition" and "the circuit's closing" for "the general debilitation of the humanities".

31. It might be thought that since Thomson insists, plausibly enough, that an event C may cause something that is over before C is over (p. 64), it would have been quicker to argue that Alpha has, in the circuit's closing, an effect that the vacuuming lacks. The circuit's closing is an effect of what is the foremost part of both Alpha and the vacuuming. But unlike Alpha, the vacuuming has the circuit's closing as a part and ipso facto not as an effect.

This would be *too* quick, however. If Alpha causes the circuit's closing and that in turn causes the remaining part of Alpha, then by the assumed transitivity of causation Alpha will cause part of itself—which is absurd. So the circuit's closing is not an effect of Alpha after all (Thomson's principle (IV) yields this conclusion directly). But this has a wacky upshot: it makes Alpha's status as a cause of the circuit's closing turn on what the circuit's closing causes *later on*. Schwartz points this out in his review of *Acts and Other Events*, 103-104; cf. section 1 of Michael Bratman, Review of *Acts and Other Events, Noûs* 16 (1982).

32. Or so an anonymous referee for *Analysis* insists.

sists of?"[33] My examples of the foregoing suggest a way. Specification of causes is typically relative to standing conditions, which may include already-caused parts of the event for which a cause is being specified. If we took Thomson's principle at its word, a partial cause of something could not be a cause of it at all. So there could not be such a thing as the straw that caused the camel's back to break. But the way we use the word "caused" suggests otherwise.

Identifying something as a cause is often motivated by a concern for having control over effects. Where control can be exercised, the counterpoint to causation is prevention. (Prevention is itself a type of causation, of course.) An effect is prevented if and only if it is not caused, and caused if and only if it is not prevented. In a situation where causing a particular effect is dependent on causing a still missing part of that effect, whatever prevents the part from occurring also prevents the effect from occurring. So by parity of reasoning we should be able to say that whatever causes the missing part to occur also thereby causes the particular effect to occur.

"We are not accustomed to talk of parts of events," says Thomson, "and have not asked ourselves what causal relations we should take the parts of an event y to have to the events that cause y."[34] The reason we don't ask ourselves this is because in our practical affairs we usually get along fine without precise answers to such questions. And I think this is reflected in our causal verbs. In the absence of explicit qualifications, "causes", "caused", and other causal verbs are vague and indeterminate as regards the question of full vs. partial. (Pragmatic circumstances can sometimes introduce precision and determinateness by way of implicature, but ordinarily such pre-

33. Thomson, *Acts and Other Events*, 63.

34. Thomson, *Acts and Other Events*, 63.

cision and determinateness has no point.) Perhaps Thomson's principle, instead of being viewed as outright false, might be better regarded as a stipulative restriction on ordinary language. Such a stipulation, to be sure, could turn out to be well motivated and highly
useful. However, examples whose interpretation depends essentially
on such stipulation have no force against a criterion that purports to
use causal terms in the ordinary way.

Another challenge to Davidson's criterion which does not rely
on causal isolation has been made by Brand. His example differs
from Thomson's in that it does not essentially involve a dis-
continuous event such as Alpha:

> Suppose that there is a causal chain in which an object first undergoes
> fission and then is reunited by a process of fusion. Assume further that
> no other object causally interacts with it during this time. There are two
> events that are occurring from the time slightly prior [sic[35]] to the
> fission to the time slightly later [sic] than the fusion, since each event
> involves distinct spatio-temporal objects. Nevertheless, these two events
> have exactly the same causes and effects.[36]

To simplify matters, let us call the prefission object "Aleph", the
fission products, respectively "Beth" and "Gimel", and the fusion
product, "Daleth". We are considering, then, the following
(simplified) causal sequence of events: Aleph's undergoing fission,
the life and times of Beth and Gimel, and the advent of Daleth.

I have redescribed Brand's example in this manner so that the
events in the sequence can be conveniently identified in terms of the
objects involved. Thus in my shorthand the causal sequence is

35. Brand has it backwards if he means to individuate these events in terms of their
objects. Before fission, as well as after fusion, there is but one object.

36. Brand, "Particulars, Events, and Actions", 137.

henceforth simply: Aleph, Beth-Gimel, and Daleth. Beth-Gimel has events Beth and Gimel as parts.

Brand gives us no argument for the claim that Beth has the same causes and effects as Gimel. Perhaps his reasoning is along these lines: since Aleph causes (for the purposes of the example, all the parts of) Beth-Gimel, Aleph causes Beth and Aleph causes Gimel. Effects, however, are more problematic. Let us assume that all the parts of Beth-Gimel are causally operative with respect to something in Daleth. Then by the principle I suggested as a replacement for Thomson's above—i.e. by (A*), which states that an event is a cause of another if it causes some of its parts and is not itself a part—we can make the move from Beth-Gimel's being a cause of Daleth to Beth's being a cause of Daleth and Gimel's being a cause of Daleth.

I now contend the following. First, that neither Beth nor Gimel is, by itself, sufficient to cause all the parts of Daleth. Secondly, that each causes at least some parts of Daleth that the other does not. A consideration that supports these contentions is the fact that it takes two to fuse and that each of Beth and Gimel makes its own unique contribution to that end.

What Brand has done is to abstract from his example at too superficial a level. One can take a causal chain and by "splitting" an intermediate event into parts, create two more causal chains whose events preserve the "is a cause of" relation. That is, from

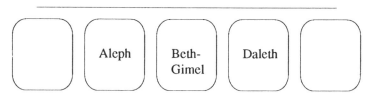

we can get the two additional chains:

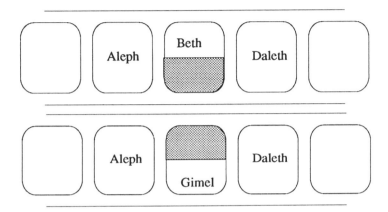

However, once this sort of event subdivision is made, we have to examine the other events in the chain more closely with respect to their parts as well. It is quite plausible that all the events that follow Beth in the causal chain could also follow Gimel. However, if I am right, this is not the same as their having all the same effects. Beth is a cause of Daleth and Gimel is a cause of Daleth, but some of the parts of Daleth that the one causes will not be among the parts the other causes. If this is so, then Beth and Gimel will not have exactly the same effects, thus coming out as distinct on Davidson's criterion.

Although Thomson's and Brand's particular examples involving events and their scattered or contiguous parts fail to invalidate Davidson's criterion of event identity, it might nonetheless be thought that that sort of reasoning could, with a little friendly tinkering, be made to yield events with the same causes and effects. I don't deny this; in fact I will show how it can be done. However, I believe that the sort of tinkering required will ipso facto ensure that there's no problem. In illustration, consider the causal chain

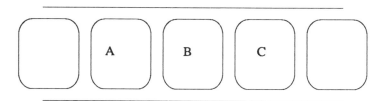

and a similar chain with a part of *B*—namely *B"*—excluded:

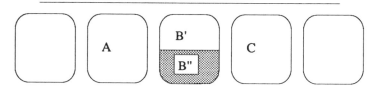

B and *B'* can have exactly the same causes and effects, provided we are willing to make a certain assumption about *B"*, viz. that *B"* is uncaused and is not itself a cause. In that event, the events *B* and *B'* would indeed have the same causes and effects. However, in making such a move we are in effect assimilating such examples to those of the isolational objection. They would then turn on the issue of causally isolated events and not merely on the relationships between events and their parts. The "part-whole" elements of the present example are unnecessary window-dressing as far as making that point is concerned.

To sum up, then, three things were accomplished in the preceding discussion of Davidson's criterion. First, it was shown that the criterion has important and interesting implications. Secondly, considerations were advanced which suggest that objections based on events alleged not to be causal relata are mistaken. Thirdly, we have shown that two initially worrying objections phrased in terms of causal chains involving events and their parts do not, after all, work.

9

CONCLUSION

9.1 Anscombe's Question Revisited

The discussion of Davidson's criterion in the preceding chapter represents the last stage in my general defence of Davidson's treatment of events. We began this essay on the identity and individuation of events with a question raised by Anscombe. Before wrapping things up, it is meet that we return to this question and, with the insight that comes with hindsight, provide an answer. Anscombe's question, it will be recalled, was this:

> Are we to say that the man who (intentionally) moves his arm, operates the pump, replenishes the water supply, poisons the inhabitants, is performing *four* actions? Or only one?[1]

In defending Davidson, I have defended an approach to the individuation of events according to which "only one" could be an acceptable answer to a transcription of Anscombe's question in some conceivable context. What I would now like to emphasize—at the

---

1. Anscombe, *Intention*, 45.

risk of belaboring the obvious—is that there is nothing that would be a correct numerical answer to *Anscombe's* question as such. This is because her example of the man who moves his arm, operates the pump, etc. just does not provide us with the information to make such a judgment.

Such factitious examples are severely and systematically under-determined, and do not compel us to any specific answer unless it is already begged. The best we can do with respect to such examples is establish that certain answers would not be precluded on logical or semantic grounds. One way we might do this, as the second last sentence suggests, is simply to build a specific answer into the example and show that this does not affect its coherency.

9.2 Individuation and Identity

In real life examples, the particular event-describing locutions employed, the descripta these locutions have in the circumstances, and (thus) the sameness and difference of these descripta, would be largely determined by the pragmatics of the situation—including the interests of the interlocuters—rather than simply the form of the locutions.

Given our interests, we individuate events differently for different purposes. This does not mean that for some purposes we may count some particular events as many and for other purposes as one. Rather it means that with different purposes prevailing, the same event-describing locution, uttered in otherwise similar circumstances, might pick out different events. *Who* describes the event often makes a big difference.

For example, a gun fetishist might pick out by "the killing" an action which would have the appropriate erotic overtones for him, say the slow squeezing of the trigger. A court prosecutor might include under that rubric a previous attempt to pull the trigger and a subsequent unjamming of the weapon, in order to underscore the malefactor's determination. The phrase "the killing" as such no more *correctly* picks out one than the other. In the first case we count the killing and the trigger-pulling as one event; in the second, as distinct events.

Hence, to put it suggestively, we can proceed from the same event-descriptions to different events, and thus different individuation of events, given our interests. Conversely, we can proceed from one and the same event to different individuations. If I go out walking in the park for my constitution, the fact that this activity is uninterrupted and is undertaken for the purpose of earning my aerobic points may lead me to consider my walking as one walk—

the one I went on to earn my aerobic points. On the other hand a civic employee collecting data on park use might choose to individuate my walking as two walks, e.g. the one through the gardens and the one along the forest trail.

Individuation does not always, of course, arise out of our particular interests of the moment. It may also be a product of habit or conditioning. Suppose a person is asked what happened on some particular occasion and he responds with some locution describing what took place, say for example, "There was a fire." The questioner presses for more information. Case one: He demands, "Tell me more about *that*." This would suggest that further information provided would be of or about *that*, i.e. the same thing the initial description was about. Case two: The questioner demands, "Tell me what *else* happened." This would suggest that the additional information would be about something *else*, other than what the initial description was about.[2]

Now these cases might be cases involving interest. In case one our questioner might have a special fascination for fires, while in case two he might be more interested in the reactions of people. On the other hand, the demand which sets the tone for individuation (assuming the informant complies) may simply be more prominent in the questioner's repertoire of responses.

Incidentally, this kind of example can also be made to illustrate the kind of indeterminateness involved in examples which rely on intuitions about locutions without consideration of pragmatics. The interesting thing to be noted here is that the informant's utterances (initial plus supplementary descriptions) might be the same in both cases one and two. In the absence of suggestive clues such as pro-

2. This example is from Beardsley, "Actions and Events: The Problem of Individuation", 265.

vided by the form of the questioner's imperatives—as in a case where the informant is making all the same utterances, but is volunteering the information without prompting—we would have no basis short of mind reading for deciding whether the individuation is as in case one or as in case two. That is, we would not be in a position to tell whether the discussion centered on one event, a fire, or on a fire and something else apart from it.

In claiming that interests and predispositions influence individuation, I do not mean to suggest, though, that individuation is entirely up to the speaker. Clearly the type of event involved also imposes some constraints on individuation. For example, there is a fair amount of leeway with respect to the composing of a jingle. That can include all the inchoate humming, finger drumming, false starts on paper, provisional bars on piano, right down to the transcription of the final note on paper. The advertising firm though might not be willing to pay for some of these when it negotiates time contracts with its jingle writers. However, with respect to a performance of this jingle there is little leeway. That begins with the first and ends with the last note.

Take another example. Depending on what happens afterwards, "making love" can begin with eye contact—for those of romantic bent, and those whose speech patterns predate the current generation. Making love in the savvy but euphemistic contemporary sense, on the other hand, begins more naturally when "what happens afterwards" begins.

What these examples indicate, then, is that event individuation is also a function of the type of event under consideration.[3]

---

3. I owe the formulation of this point and the inspiration for the preceding examples to John Heintz.

Now in the light of the remarks I have made about the indeterminateness of event-talk and relativity of event individuation, it might be thought that I have thereby in effect (1) undermined Davidson's criterion, that I have (2) implicitly suggested alternative, pragmatic-cum-semantic criteria for event identity, and that I have (3) done (1) by doing (2).

Not so. What I have suggested is that depending on the types of events involved, pragmatic considerations such as speakers' interests and purposes will influence what is picked out or left out by event-describing expressions, and that therefore even utterances of the same expression may not identify the same event. What I have not suggested is that such considerations would be decisive in establishing the sameness or difference of events in every case. So (2) cannot be correct.

Furthermore, there is no suggestion that in those cases where pragmatic considerations do suffice to establish sameness or difference, we will have established something incompatible with Davidson's criterion. There may be a hint, in what I have said, that pragmatic evidence is sometimes easier to come by than causal knowledge. That, however, indicates an epistemological difficulty in applying the criterion. It does not constitute a reason for worrying about its status as a metaphysical truth. There is no necessary conflict between the use of pragmatic considerations and Davidson's criterion, and thus (1) is not correct.

That these claims of mine are entirely within the spirit with which Davidson himself views his criterion is evident in these remarks:

> Perhaps sameness of causal relations is the only condition always sufficient to establish sameness of events (sameness of location in space and time may be another). But this should not be taken to mean that the only way of establishing, or supporting, a claim that two events are

identical is by giving causal evidence. On the contrary, logic alone, or logic plus physics, or almost anything else, may help do the job, depending on the descriptions provided.[4]

What exactly is the connection between Davidson's criterion of event identity and the matter of event individuation? The answer has, I think, already been intimated in the preceding, but in order for it to be clearly stated some general remarks must first be made.

When as language users we deal with events at the level of what I have been calling "event-talk", we are also engaged in making classifications or relying on previously made classifications. Individuating events at this level involves picking them out by means of expressions which identify or characterize them as being of a certain type (in the most general sense). For example, using the expression "the shooting" to refer to an event has the effect of classifying that event as a shooting. Individuation at the level of classifying and picking out is something that we can do without a concern for counting.

Individuating events in terms of number, on the other hand, involves making judgments of a higher order than classification. At this level individuation will involve judging whether the events we have classified are the same or distinct, and then enumerating them. Such judgments are made on the basis of available information, and as Davidson says, almost anything may help do the job. Semantic considerations are for example sufficient to establish that something classified as an eating cannot also be classified as a shooting. I previously suggested some pragmatic considerations that will help in other cases. And information about causes and effects will of course also aid judgment here.

---

4. Davidson, "The Individuation of Events", 231-232 <179-180>.

A criterion of identity for events, in our sense, is a statement of necessary and sufficient conditions for the truth of identity statements of the form "$x = y$". In the ideal case, a criterion of identity will also be an individuating criterion at both levels of individuation. Identity criteria for formal entities such as classes and numbers, when supplanted with a few axioms, could make individuation to a routine. Such criteria however also have a conventional character—they simultaneously introduce odd uses of "same" and invent entities for them to apply to.[5]

The situation with respect to identity criteria for events is different. Not only will the identity conditions in the definiens be *post facto* as far as the reference of the terms in the definiendum is concerned, but there is in addition no guarantee that the world will co-operate in releasing the information required to apply the criterion. In the case of Davidson's causal criterion, we may not in a particular case have the causal knowledge required to use it to make a good decision about sameness or difference.

Davidson's criterion is a general criterion of individuation in principle, but not in practice. It could work as an unqualified principle of individuation only for a Being—and such a Being deserves to be capitalized—omniscient in matters causal. None of this is to deny, though, that enough causal knowledge for making sound judgments of individuation is in fact available in many cases.

In the light of the preceding, the connection between individuation and the criterion of identity can now be stated. It is this. The criterion of identity purports to specify a metaphysical standard—in terms of the fewest properties, and so at once more elegant and wieldy than Leibnitz's law—with respect to which particular

5. Here I am borrowing from Prior, *Objects of Thought*, chapter 4, section 5.

judgments of sameness or difference, however arrived at, will be either correct or incorrect.

If Davidson's criterion holds up, *der logische Raum* for events will be a causal grid.

BIBLIOGRAPHY

Alston, William P. "Ziff's Semantic Analysis." *Journal of Philosophy* 59 (1962): 5-20.

Annas, Julia. "Davidson and Anscombe on 'the same action'." *Mind* 75 (1976): 251-257.

Anscombe, G.E.M. *Intention.* 2nd ed. Oxford: Basil Blackwell, 1976.

———. "Under a Description." *Noûs* 13 (1979): 219-233.

Aune, Bruce. *Reason and Action.* Dordrecht-Holland: D. Reidel Publishing Co., 1977.

Austin, J.L. *How to Do Things With Words.* Edited by J.O. Urmson. New York: Oxford University Press, 1968.

Baier, Kurt. See Toulmin and Baier.

Beardsley, Monroe C. "Actions and Events: The Problem of Individuation." *American Philosophical Quarterly* 12 (1975): 263-276.

Bennett, Jonathan. "Shooting, Killing and Dying." *Canadian Journal of Philosophy* 2 (1973): 315-323.

Bloom, Allan. *The Closing of the American Mind*. New York: Touchstone Books/Simon and Schuster, Inc., 1988.

Brand, Myles. Review of *A Theory of Human Action*, by Alvin I. Goldman. *Journal of Philosophy* 69 (1972): 249-257.

————. "Particulars, Events, and Actions." In *Action Theory*, edited by M. Brand and D. Walton. Dordrecht-Holland: D. Reidel Publishing Co., 1976.

————. "Reply to Martin." In *Action Theory*, edited by M. Brand and D. Walton. Dordrecht-Holland: D. Reidel Publishing Co., 1976.

Bratman, Michael. "Individuation and Action." *Philosophical Studies* 33 (1978): 367-375.

————. Review of *Acts and Other Events*, by Judith Jarvis Thomson. *Noûs* 16 (1982): 467-473.

Bridgman, P.W. *A Sophisticate's Primer of Relativity*. Middletown, Connecticut: Wesleyan University Press, 1962.

Bunge, Mario. *Causality*. Cambridge, Massachusetts: Harvard University Press, 1959.

————. *Causality*. 3rd ed. New York: Dover Publications, Inc., 1979.

Butler, R.J. See R.M. Martin et al.

Cartwright, Richard. "Scattered Objects." In *Philosophical Papers*. Cambridge, Massachusetts: The M.I.T. Press, 1987.

Castañeda, Hector-Neri. 'Comments on D. Davidson's "The Logical Form of Action Sentences".' In *The Logic of Decision and Action,* edited by Nicholas Rescher. University of Pittsburgh Press, 1966.

————. "Intensionality and Identity in Human Action and Philosophical Method", *Noûs* 13 (1979): 235-260.

Chisholm, Roderick M. 'Comments on D. Davidson's "The Logical Form of Action Sentences".' In *The Logic of Decision and Action,* edited by Nicholas Rescher. Unversity of Pittsburgh Press, 1966.

———. "Events and Propositions." *Noûs* 4 (1970): 15-24.

———. "States of Affairs Again." *Noûs* 5 (1971): 335-349.

———. "Problems of Identity." In *Identity and Individuation,* edited by Milton K. Munitz. New York Unversity Press, 1971.

Clark, Romane. "Concerning the Logic of Predicate Modifiers." *Noûs* 4 (1970): 311-335.

Cresswell, M.J. "Adverbs and Events." *Synthese* 28 (1974): 455-481.

———. "Why Objects Exist but Events Occur." *Studia Logica* 45 (1986): 371-375.

D'Arcy, Eric. *Human Acts.* Oxford: The Clarendon Press, 1963.

Davidson, Donald. "Action, Reasons, and Causes." *Journal of Philosophy* 60 (1963): 685-700.

———. "Causal Relations." *Journal of Philosophy* 64 (1967): 691-703.

———. "The Logical Form of Action Sentences." In *The Logic of Decision and Action,* edited by Nicholas Rescher. Pittsburgh: University of Pittsburgh Press, 1967.

———. "Reply to Comments." In *The Logic of Decision and Action,* edited by Nicholas Rescher, Pittsburgh: University of Pittsburgh Press, 1967.

———. "The Individuation of Events." In *Essays in Honor of Carl G. Hempel,* edited by N. Rescher et al. Dordrecht-Holland: D. Reidel Publishing Co., 1969 .

———. "Action and Reaction." *Inquiry* 13 (1970): 140-148.

———. "Events as Particulars." *Noûs* 4 (1970): 25-32.

———. "Eternal vs. Ephemeral Events." *Noûs* 5 (1971): 335-349.

————. *Essays on Actions and Events.* Oxford: Clarendon Press, 1980.

Davis, Lawrence H. "Individuation of Actions." *Journal of Philosophy* 67 (1970): 520-530.

Dretske, Fred I. "Referring to Events." In *Studies in the Philosophy of Language*, Midwest Studies in Philosophy, 2. Morris, Minnesota: University of Minnesota Press, (1977): 90-99.

Elliot, Robert and Michael Smith. "Individuating Actions: A Reply to McCullagh and Thalberg." *Australasian Journal of Philosophy* 55 (1976): 209-212.

Feldman, Richard H., and Edward Wierenga. "Thalberg on the Irreducibility of Events." *Analysis* 39 (1979): 11-16.

Francis, Diane. "Lynden Pindling's day in court." *Maclean's*, 20 June 1988, p. 9.

Freedman, Daniel Z., and Peter von Nieuwenhuizen. "Supergravity and the Unification of the Laws of Physics." *Scientific American* 238 (February 1978): 126-143.

Fulcher, Lewis P., Johann Rafelski, and Abraham Klein. "The Decay of the Vacuum." *Scientific American* 241 (December 1979): 150-159.

Geach, Peter T. *Reference and Generality.* Emended Edition. Ithaca, N.Y.: Cornell University Press, 1968.

George, Tim. "Action, Behavior and Bodily Movement: A Sketch of a Theory of Action." *Auslegung* 5 (1977): 43-57.

Goldman, Alvin I. *A Theory of Human Action.* Englewood Cliffs, New Jersey: Prentice-Hall, Inc., 1970.

————. "The Individuation of Action." *Journal of Philosophy* 68 (1971): 761-774.

Goodman, Nelson. "A World of Individuals." In *Contemporary Readings in Logical Theory*, edited by Irving M. Copi and James A. Gould. New York: The MacMillan Company, 1967.

——. *The Structure of Appearance.* 3rd ed., Boston Studies in the Philosophy of Science, 53. Dordrecht-Holland: D. Reidel Publishing Co., 1977.

Gjelsvik, Olav. "A Note on Objects and Events." *Analysis* 48 (1988): 15-17.

Haeseker, Fred. "Killer sentenced to life for 'mercy strangling'." *The Calgary Herald,* 25 March 1977.

Helm, Paul. 'Are "Cambridge" Changes Non-events?' *Analysis* 35 (1975): 140-144.

Hempel, Carl G. *Aspects of Scientific Explanation and Other Essays in the Philosophy of Science.* New York: The Free Press, 1965.

Horgan, Terence. "The Case Against Events." *Philosophical Review* 87 (1978): 28-47.

Jobe, Evan K. "Temporal Predication and Identity." *Australasian Journal of Philosophy* 54 (1976): 65-71.

Kac, Michael B. "Action and Result: Two Aspects of Predication in English." In *Syntax and Semantics,* 1, edited by John P. Kimbal. New York: Seminar Press, 1972.

——. "Reply to McCawley." In *Syntax and Semantics,* 1, edited by John P. Kimbal. New York: Seminar Press, 1972.

Katz, Bernard D. "Is the Causal Criterion of Event-Identity Circular?" *Australasian Journal of Philosophy* 56 (1978): 225-229.

——. "Kim on Events." *Philosophical Review* 87 (1978): 427-441.

Kim, Jaegwon. "Events and Their Descriptions: Some Considerations." In *Essays in Honor of Carl G. Hemple,* edited by Nicholas Rescher et al. Dordrecht-Holland: D. Reidel Publishing Co., 1969.

——. "Noncausal Connections." *Noûs* 8 (1974): 41-52.

——. "Events as Property Exemplifications." In *Action Theory*, edited by M. Brand and D. Walton. Dordrecht-Holland: D. Reidel Publishing Co., 1976.

——. "Causation, Emphasis, and Events." *Midwest Studies in Philosophy* 2 (1977): 100-103.

Kubara, Michael. "Acrasia, Human Agency and Normative Psychology." *Canadian Journal of Philosophy* 5 (1975): 215-232.

——. "Strictly Speaking and Other Actions." Commentary on Karl Pfeifer, "Time, Death and Event Identity", read at the Annual Meeting of the Canadian Philosophical Association, University of Saskatchewan, 4 June 1979.

Lemmon, E.J. 'Comments on D. Davidson's "The Logical Form of Action Sentences".' In *The Logic of Decision and Action*, edited by Nicholas Rescher. University of Pittsburgh Press, 1966.

Lombard, Brian Lawrence. "Chisholm and Davidson on Events and Counterfacutals." *Philosophia* 7 (1978): 512-522.

MacDonald, C.A. "On the Unifier-Multiplier Controversy." *Canadian Journal of Philosophy* 8 (1978): 707-714.

Martin, R.M. *Belief, Existence and Meaning*. New York University Press, 1969.

——. *Logic, Language and Metaphysics*. New York University Press, 1971.

——. "Events and Actions: Some Comments on Brand and Kim." In *Action Theory*, edited by M. Brand and D. Walton. Dordrecht-Holland: D. Reidel Publishing Co., 1976.

Martin, R.M. et al. "Symposium: On Events and Event-Descriptions." In *Fact and Existence*, edited by Joseph Margolis. Oxford: Basil Blackwell, 1969.

McCawley, James D. "Kac and Shibatani on the Grammar of Killing." In *Syntax and Semantics,* 1, edited by John P. Kimball. New York: Seminar Press, 1972.

McCullagh, C.B. "The Individuation of Actions and Acts." *Australasian Journal of Philosophy* 54 (1976): 133-139.

Moravcsik, J. "Strawson and Ontological Priority." In *Analytical Philsophy, Second Series,* edited by R.J. Butler. Oxford: Basil Blackwell, 1968.

Nietzsche, Friedrich. *On the Genealogy of Morals.* Translated by Walter Kaufmann and R.J. Hollingdale, in *On the Genealogy of Morals and Ecce Homo,* edited by Walter Kaufmann. New York: Vintage Books, 1967.

Pfeifer, Karl. "Davidson's Criterion of Event Identity." Paper read at the seminar on Science and Philosophy, Interuniverzitetski Centar za Postdiplomski Studij, Dubrovnik, 5 April 1979.

———. "Time, Death, and Event Identity." Paper read at the Conference of the Canadian Philosophical Association, University of Saskatchewan, 4 June 1979.

Prior, A.N. *Objects of Thought.* Edited by P.T. Geach and A.J.P. Kenny. Oxford: Clarendon Press, 1971.

Queneau, Raymond. *The Flight of Icarus.* Translated by Barbara Wright. London: Calder & Boyers, 1973.

Quine, Willard Van Orman. *Word and Object.* Cambridge, Massachusetts: The M.I.T. Press, 1960.

———. "Identity, ostension, and hypostasis." In *From a Logical Point of View,* Second Edition, revised. New York: Harper & Row, Publishers, 1963.

———. *Set Theory and Its Logic.* Revised Edition. Cambridge, Massachusetts: The Belknap Press of Harvard University Press, 1969.

Reichenbach, Hans. *Elements of Symbolic Logic.* New York: The Macmillan Company, 1947.

Rescher, Nicholas. "Aspects of Action." In *The Logical of Decision and Action,* edited by Nicholas Rescher. Pittsburgh University Press, 1966.

Richards, Norvin. *"E Pluribus Unum*: A Defence of Davidson's Individuation of Action." *Philosophical Studies* 29 (1976): 191-198.

Ripley, Charles. "The Individuation of Actions: *A Fatal Blow to the Standard Approach.*" Paper read at the Western Conference of the Canadian Philosophical Association, Winnipeg, 1977.

Salmon, Wesley C. See R.M. Martin et al.

Scheffler, Israel. *The Anatomy of Inquiry.* New York: Alfred A. Knopf, 1969.

Scherweghs, G. *Present-Day English Syntax.* London: Longmans, 1959.

Schwartz, Stephen P. Review of *Acts and Other Events,* by Judith Jarvis Thomson. *Philosophical Review* 88 (1979): 100-105.

Schwayder, D.S. *The Stratification of Behaviour.* London: Routledge & Kegan Paul, 1965.

Shibatani, Masayoshi. "Three Reasons for Not Deriving 'Kill' from 'Cause to Die' in Japanese." In *Syntax and Semantics,* 1, edited by John P. Kimball. New York: Seminar Press, 1972.

Simpson, Evan. "Actions and Extensions." *American Philosophical Quarterly* 7 (1970): 349-356.

Smith, Michael. See Elliot and Smith.

Sparshott, F.E. "Franciscus." In *Looking for Philosophy.* Montreal and London: McGill-Queens University Press, 1972.

Stalnaker, Robert C. "Events, Periods, and Institutions in Historians' Language." *History and Theory* 5 (1967): 159-179.

Stenner, Alfred J. "Toward a Theory of Event Identity." *Philosophy of Science* 41 (1974): 65-83.

Strawson, P.F. *Individuals*. London: Methuen & Co. Ltd., 1969.

Sweet, Henry. *A New English Grammer, Logical and Historical: Part 1*. Oxford: Clarendon Press, 1900.

Sweet, Henry. *A New English Grammer, Logical and Historical: Part 2*. Oxford: Clarendon Press, 1958.

Taylor, Barry. "States of Affairs." In *Truth and Meaning: Essays in Semantics,* edited by Gareth Evans and John McDowell. Oxford: Clarendon Press, 1976.

Taylor, Richard. "Causation." In *The Encyclopedia of Philosophy*, Reprint Edition, edited by Paul Edwards. New York: Macmillan Publishing Co., Inc. & The Free Press, 1972. Vol. 2, 56-66.

Thalberg, Irving. "Singling Out Actions, Their Properties and Components." *Journal of Philosophy* 68 (1971): 781-787.

———. "The Irreducibility of Events." *Analysis* 38 (1978): 1-9.

Thomson, Judith Jarvis. "The Time of a Killing." *Journal of Philosophy* 68 (1971): 115-132.

———. "Individuating Actions." *Journal of Philosophy* 68 (1971): 774-781.

———. *Acts and Other Events*. Ithaca, N.Y.: Cornell University Press, 1977.

Tiles, J.E. "Davidson's Criterion of Event Identity." *Analysis* 36 (1976): 185-187.

Toulmin, S.E. and K. Baier. "On Describing." In *Philosophy and Ordinary Language,* edited by Charles E. Caton. Chicago: University of Illinois Press, 1963.

Trenholm, Russell. "Doing Without Events." *Canadian Journal of Philosophy* 8 (1978): 173-185.

Van Fraasen, Bas C. *An Introduction to the Philosophy of Time and Space.* New York: Random House, 1970.

Ware, Robert. "Acts and Action." *Journal of Philsophy* 70 (1973): 401-418.

White, Morton. *Foundations of Historical Knowledge.* New York: Harper and Row, 1965.

Wierenga, Edward. "Chisholm on States of Affairs." *Australasian Journal of Philosophy* 54 (1976): 148-152.

Wierenga, Edward. See Feldman and Wierenga, 1979.

Wilson, N.L. "Space, Time, and Individuals." *Journal of Philsophy* 52 (1955): 589-598.

———. "Facts, Events and Their Identity Conditions." *Philosophical Studies* 25 (1974): 303-321.

Woods, M.J. "Identity and Individuation." In *Analytical Philsophy, Second Series,* edited by R.J. Butler. Oxford: Basil Blackwell, 1968.

Yagisawa, T. "Counterfacutal Analysis of Causation and Kim's Examples." *Analysis* 39 (1979): 100-105.

Ziff, Paul. *Semantic Analysis.* Ithaca, N.Y.: Cornell University Press, 1960.

INDEX

Page numbers in italics refer to footnotes.

12, 37, 46, 47, 81, 94, 133;
problem, 24, 37, 40, 41;
reasoning, 85
Relations, 24; explanatory, 153
Richards, Norvin, 93
    E Pluribus Unum, *80, 93*
Scheffler, Israel, (The Anatomy of
    Inquiry), *70*
Schwartz, Stephen P., *170, 171,*
    173
Shibatani, Masayoshi, *78*
Shooting-killing, 10, 12, 19-20,
    22-23, 30-32, 34, 65, 78-79, 107
Simple generation, 18-19, 23, 27,
    44, 53, 57
Sparshott, F.E., *126*
Spatial Inclusion, 55
Stern, Cindy D., (The Prospects for
    Elimination), *139*
Sum-individuals, 137
Symmetry, 25
Taylor, Richard,(Causation), *168*
Temporal, 33; actions, 31-34, 36;
    argument, 97; inclusion, 55;
    objection, 13, 30, 32-33, 35, 37,
    47, 66, 95, 96, 111-112, 133;
    ordering, 167; problem, 12, 30,
    32, 37, 40, 66; relations, 35;
    requirement, 33-34; restriction,
    33, 37;
Thalberg, Irving, 5, 6, *118*
    Singling Out Actions, *5, 122,*
    128
Thomson, Judith Jarvis, 6, 67-69,
    81-84, *94,* 96-99, 169-177
    Acts and Other Events, *68,*
    169, 171, 173, 174
    Individuating Actions, *81, 83*
    The Time of a Killing ,*67, 97,*
    99, 105
Tiles, J.E., (Davidson's Criterion),
    160

Timeless existence, 151
Times, 151
Transitivity, 17, 29, 36, 45, 58, 90
Types of events, 183
Uncaused events, 166
Unifier-multiplier dispute, 5-6,
    113, 117-118, 122, 125, 127,
    131, 134, 136, 139-140
Unifiers, 2, 5-6, 8-11, 13, 21, 37,
    40, 118-119, 121, 125, 131,
    133, 135-136, 140, 152-154
Unifying account, 60, 62-63, 87,
    118-119, 121-125, 131, 133-137,
    139-140, 152-153
Vacuuming (example), 169-173
Vacuums, 149
Von Nieuwenhuizen, Peter,
    (Supergravity), *148*
Waterfalls, 141-142, 147
White, Morton, (Foundations of
    Historical Knowledge), *73*
Wilson, N.L., (Facts, Events and
    Their Identity Conditions), *160*
Zundel, Ernst, *68*

Thomas William Segady

VALUES, NEO-KANTIANISM, AND THE DEVELOPMENT OF WEBERIAN METHODOLOGY

American University Studies: Series V (Philosophy). Vol. 41
ISBN 0-8204-0506-X   184 pages   hardback US $ 28.00*

*Recommended price – alterations reserved

The works of Max Weber have generated a most promising interest in the social sciences with regard to his contribution to contemporary thought. While many of his substantive insights have been recognized, the attention accorded his methodological works has been comparatively scant, and often is a mere reflection of the scattered manner in which Weber himself often pursued this topic. Despite the many confusions and contradictions in Weber's methodological thought, a Weberian methodological program can be constructed from his writings. By focusing on Weber's emphasis on the study of values as developed within a neo-Kantian framework, the development of Weber's methodological thought is outlined, and out of this a methodological program consistent with Weberian principles is proposed. Thus, the argument is made that Weber's methodological works are not merely of historical interest, but inform the ongoing debate over the appropriate methodological orientation of the social sciences.

". . . a solid contribution to intellectual history in general and the History of Sociological Theory in particular . . . beyond the usual treatment of Weber." (William H. Key, Professor Emeritus University of Denver)

 PETER LANG PUBLISHING, INC.
62 West 45th Street
USA – New York, NY 10036

Appelbaum, David

THE INTERPENETRATING REALITY
Bringing the Body to Touch

New York, Berne, Frankfurt/M., Paris, 1988.
American University Studies: Series 5, Philosophy. Vol. 44
ISBN 0-8204-0556-6   196 pages   hardback $ 30.50/sFr. 42.60

The Interpenetrating Reality is a philosophical investigation of what inhibits a fresh perception of the world. It explores the dulling effect of habit on tactile contact with the body. A disharmonized cognitive function which keeps the mind preoccupied is analyzed. Embodiment or an incarnate state is studied as an alternative avenue to the act of perception. The body itself as an organ of perception provides the keynote of the examination.

Contents: A study of organic life as perception – The body's role in the act of perception – The tactile sense as offering a new approach to our sense of reality.

PETER LANG PUBLISHING, INC.
62 West 45th Street
USA – New York, NY 10036

Allen, Paul III

PROOF OF MORAL OBLIGATION IN TWENTIETH-CENTURY PHILOSOPHY

New York, Berne, Frankfurt/M., Paris, 1988.
American University Studies: Philosophy, Series 5, Vol. 45
ISBN 0-8204-0568-X   200 pages   hardback $ 31.65/sFr. 44.30

Since Plato's time, philosophers have concentrated on developing moral theories to guide our actions. They have said we ought to act to maximize happiness; we ought to act to fulfill human potential; etc. But all of them have largely ignored a key question: Regardless of *which* acts are morally obligatory, *can moral obligation as such be proven?*

Early in his book, Allen clarifies what sort of demonstration or justification can suffice as a proof that we are subject to moral obligation. He analyzes some twentieth-century ethical theories which initially appear to serve as such a demonstration. Next, he examines at length the theory of contemporary English philosopher R.M. Hare. And finally, he reworks Hare's ideas into a complete proof that we are bound by moral obligation.

Philosophers should value this book because it brings to light and defines a neglected but critical problem, and develops an innovative, thought-provoking solution. Serious students, too, will find it helpful because it provides a clearly written historical study of a central theme in twentieth-century ethics.

Contents: A historical analysis of the ethics of Moore, Prichard, Ayer, Toulmin, and R.M. Hare, with a lengthy study of Hare. Goal is to find a *proof* of moral obligation. Hare's theory combined with insights from Alan Gewirth finally does yield a proof of moral obligation.

PETER LANG PUBLISHING, INC.
62 West 45th Street
USA – New York, NY 10036